Privileged Moments

Books by Jeffrey Meyers

BIOGRAPHY

A Fever at the Core: The Idealist in Politics
Married to Genius
Katherine Mansfield
The Enemy: A Biography of Wyndham Lewis
Hemingway
Manic Power: Robert Lowell and His Circle
D. H. Lawrence
Joseph Conrad
Edgar Allan Poe: His Life and Legacy
Scott Fitzgerald
Edmund Wilson
Robert Frost
Bogart: A Life in Hollywood
Gary Cooper: American Hero
Privileged Moments: Encounters with Writers
Orwell: Wintry Conscience of a Generation

CRITICISM

Fiction and the Colonial Experience
The Wounded Spirit: T. E. Lawrence's Seven Pillars of Wisdom
A Reader's Guide to George Orwell
Painting and the Novel
Homosexuality and Literature
D. H. Lawrence and the Experience of Italy
Disease and the Novel
The Spirit of Biography
Hemingway: Life into Art

BIBLIOGRAPHY

T. E. Lawrence: A Bibliography
Catalogue of the Library of the Late Siegfried Sassoon
George Orwell: An Annotated Bibliography of Criticism

EDITED COLLECTIONS

George Orwell: The Critical Heritage
Hemingway: The Critical Heritage
Robert Lowell: Interviews and Memoirs

EDITED COLLECTIONS OF ORIGINAL ESSAYS

Wyndham Lewis by Roy Campbell
Wyndham Lewis: A Revaluation
D. H. Lawrence and Tradition
The Legacy of D. H. Lawrence
The Craft of Literary Biography
The Biographer's Art
T. E. Lawrence: Soldier, Writer, Legend
Graham Greene: A Revaluation

Privileged Moments

Encounters with Writers

Jeffrey Meyers

THE UNIVERSITY OF WISCONSIN PRESS

The University of Wisconsin Press
2537 Daniels Street
Madison, Wisconsin 53718

3 Henrietta Street
London WC2E 8LU, England

1   3   5   4   2

Printed in the United States of America

Library of Congress Cataloging-in-Publication Data

Meyers, Jeffrey.
Privileged moments : encounters with writers /
Jeffrey Meyers.
pp.   cm.
Includes index.
ISBN 0-299-16940-5 (alk. paper)
1. Authors, American—20th century—Biography.   2. Authors,
English—20th century—Biography.   3. Meyers, Jeffrey—
Friends and associates.   I. Title.
PS129 .M49   2000
810.9′005—dc21   00-008609

Contents

Preface

The force of a gifted and imaginative personality is compelling and seductive, and writers are enchanters. Once under an author's spell, I wanted to learn everything about his life. My biographical investigations have sometimes led to friendships, which are the subject of this book. Meeting the authors described here taught me much more than I could learn in libraries. I admired their art and sought them out, visited and corresponded with them, collected their books and taught them in my classes. They were all great talkers, and I kept a record of their conversation. They enjoyed my enthusiasm for their work and shared my literary passions. I valued their encouragement and the filial relationships that sometimes sprang up between us.

This book is part intellectual autobiography, part personal account of eight authors, born between 1915 and 1932: what they looked like, how they lived, and what they said. In this book I discuss Allen Ginsberg's views of Pound and Lawrence, James Dickey's take on Lowell and Jarrell, the poet Ed Dorn's attitude to his fatal illness, the creation of Arthur Miller's plays and the filming of *The Misfits* and *The Crucible*, Rebecca West's quarrel with Iris Murdoch and the gradual effects of Iris's Alzheimer's disease, V. S. Naipaul's extensive comments on the meaning of his work as well as his manipulative character and attempt to create an invulnerable public persona, Francis King's tempestuous homosexual adventures, J. F. Powers's singular vision of life, his deep-rooted grief and devastating reaction to his wife's death.

In all our conversations and correspondence, I was most curious about the creative process, the relation between the authors' lives and their art, the public image and the real self. They gave me many insights into their profession: how sensitive to criticism they were; how they advanced their careers and achieved fame; how feuds and quarrels started and ended; how reviews were written and prizes awarded;

how they struggled financially and went on writing despite illnesses and mental problems, problematic marriages and agonizing love affairs. Each chapter of this living literary history—with firsthand knowledge and detailed description of his life, character, and opinions—contains an intimate portrait of an artist.

Privileged Moments

1

Allen Ginsberg and James Dickey

Allen Ginsberg
1926   born in New Jersey
1949   graduates from Columbia University
1956   *Howl*
1961   *Kaddish*
1974   begins teaching summer school at Naropa Institute in Boulder, Colorado
1997   dies in New York City

James Dickey
1923   born in Georgia
1942–46   serves in Army Air Corps
1949   graduates from Vanderbilt
1962   *Drowning with Others*
1965   *Buckdancer's Choice*
1970   *Deliverance*
1997   dies in South Carolina

I

In 1997 America lost two of its finest poets: James Dickey died in January, Allen Ginsberg in April. These poets—rabbi and redneck—were opposites in almost every way. The gentle, sweet-tempered Ginsberg spoke rapidly with a New York accent. Born in New Jersey in 1926, he was a Jewish, homosexual, drug-taking Buddhist. Physically unattractive, unathletic, and intensely urban, he had been a leading protester against the war in Vietnam. The tough and fiercely competitive Dickey spoke with a southern drawl. Born in Atlanta in 1923, he was a WASPy, heterosexual, heavy-drinking rationalist. A handsome college athlete

3

and outdoor sportsman, he'd fought in World War II and was recalled for the Korean War.

Ginsberg, who looked like Yasser Arafat without the speckled head shawl, had a huge bald dome, blubbery lips, and a shaggy beard. Beneath the unkempt appearance, thick horn-rimmed glasses, and soft brown eyes was a kindly uncle and holy sage. Dickey, a big bearish man, built like Wallace Stevens and Ted Roethke, had an overwhelming physical presence. About six feet, four inches tall and weighing near 300 pounds, he was a huge whale, beached on the Carolina coast. On our second meeting his pale blue eyes, broad nose, large and slightly gapped front teeth, and jowly face were topped by a strange hair transplant that broke over his skull in a furry wave.

Ginsberg lived in a modest flat in New York's East Village. Dickey's flashy suburban spread on a man-made lake outside Columbia, South Carolina, with a big Cadillac in the driveway, was more like an ad executive's house than a poet's. Ginsberg was more subtle, Dickey more open. The former shuffled around and chuckled quietly to himself; the latter strutted about and had a convulsive laugh. Allen I associated with incense, Jim with beer. Unlike Yukio Mishima—who said, "I behave normally, but I'm sick inside"—Ginsberg and Dickey were perfectly sound in the head but sometimes carried on like wild men. For these poets, as for Blake, the road to excess led to the palace of wisdom. Ginsberg wrote in the spontaneous, loose, long-lined tradition of Walt Whitman and William Carlos Williams. The more technically skilled Dickey followed the lyrical, meditative line of Emerson and Roethke.

I'd first heard Ginsberg read his poetry, chant mantras, and play the harmonium in Boston in the late 1960s, and was surprised by how much more dramatic and moving "Howl" and "Kaddish" were when he read them aloud. He was tender on stage with his father, also a poet, in Boulder in the 1970s. He was still a great performer in Berkeley in the 1990s, and when I tried to take some English friends up to meet him, I found it impossible to step through the new generation of admirers densely packed on the floor.

I first met Allen in the spring of 1982, when I was teaching English at the University of Colorado and he was living in Boulder and teaching poetry at the Buddhist Naropa Institute. The cranes, as they said, "had settled on the lake" and Boulder had become the center of American Buddhism. John Steinbeck's son was a personal dresser to the Rinpoche (a lesser Dalai Lama), who had recently paralyzed himself by drunkenly driving his car into a store front. The Naropans had also been convulsed by scandal when William Merwin's gorgeous Polynesian girlfriend was molested and nearly raped by the Rinpoche's followers. Much of this is recounted in Tom Clark's lively polemical pamphlet, *The Great Naropa Poetry Wars* (1980). When I asked a disciple if, as rumored, the holy man slept with his students, she quickly replied, "He has the smallest prick in Boulder, but makes the most of it."

Allen himself confided that he did his best teaching while in bed with his students. He came up with the engaging if impractical suggestion that the flaky and free-wheeling Naropa Institute exchange students, courses, and credits with the University of Colorado. It would have been quite amusing to propose this to the straitlaced Board of Regents. Despite his appearance and reputation, Ginsberg—Lionel Trilling's straight-A student at Columbia—was not at all crazy, but lucid and intelligent. For all his dabbling in Eastern mysticism, he'd been instinctively right in the 1960s about the genocidal war in Vietnam and the diabolical machinations of the FBI and CIA. It took Robert McNamara, the secretary of defense, more than thirty years to grasp what Allen knew while the war was raging.

Our first meeting, in May 1982, took place, appropriately enough for two transplanted easterners, at the New York Delicatessen on Pearl Street in Boulder. Kind, likable, and easily approachable, Ginsberg did not act like a great man: we both knew who he was. He loved to talk and gave me his full attention. Having published a life of Wyndham Lewis in 1980, I was then pondering a life of Pound—or at the least the "good," early Pound. Since Allen was the only person within two thousand miles who had known Ole Ez, I was eager to talk to him.

Ginsberg had met the thin, springy, sinewy eighty-two-year-old Pound in Venice in October 1967. He found the poet benevolent yet indifferent, impersonal yet attentive. Having said many evil things in the past, Pound had now fallen silent, and Ginsberg was impressed by his poignant humanity. During their encounter Pound recanted his anti-Semitism and called it a "stupid suburban prejudice." By contrast, his companion, Olga Rudge, was rather grand, cultured, sympathetic, intelligent, and Poundcentric. Ginsberg, Pound, and Hemingway had the same Italian translator, Fernanda Pivano, and Pound's follower Robert Duncan also lived in Venice. Ginsberg traced the school of Ez from Duncan, Basil Bunting, and Louis Zukofsky to George Oppen, Charles Reznikoff, and Carl Rakosi. Ginsberg had also visited Céline in 1958 and thus had met the two most notorious anti-Semites in Europe.

Ginsberg was also illuminating about Pound's politics and poetry. James Angleton, a counter-intelligence agent in Italy during World War II (who also lived in Boulder), had told him that Pound's infamous cage in Pisa had protected him against the Partisans. I countered that since Pound had been arrested by the Partisans and closely guarded by the American army, the degrading cage wasn't strictly necessary. Ginsberg thought there had been a benevolent arrangement on both sides, concocted by Eliot, MacLeish, and Saint-John Perse, to declare Pound insane so the government wouldn't have to try and execute him as a traitor. He mentioned that the St. Elizabeth's psychiatrist E. Fuller Torrey, who had access to Pound's medical records, published an article in the November 1981 issue of *Psychology Today* arguing that the government had wrongly saved a traitor's life.

We then got on to Pound's confession that he could not make the *Cantos* cohere and to whether that meandering museum of a poem had a structural unity. Ginsberg thought it was a discrete, vivid apparition of thought forms, a model of the mind that conveyed, over half a century, the dramatic development of his states of mental consciousness. He compared it to Wordsworth's *Prelude*, but said that it had no real literary parallel as intellectual autobiography. The *Cantos* did not provide an adequate answer to the social problems, like usury, that it pretended to consider, but failed only when compared to Pound's original, ideal conception.

Our talk then drifted on to Lionel Trilling and Randall Jarrell. Ginsberg denied that he had inspired the brilliant and insane Ferdinand Tertan in Trilling's fine story "Of This Time, of That Place" (1943). He thought Trilling was not a great teacher, as Raymond Weaver and Mark Van Doren were, but he'd been kind to Ginsberg and had taken a personal interest in his welfare. Jarrell liked Gregory Corso's poetry, and had invited both Corso and Jack Kerouac to stay with him in Washington in 1956 when he was poetry consultant at the Library of Congress. Kerouac later portrayed Jarrell as Varnum Random in *Desolation Angels* (1965). That afternoon Ginsberg inscribed my copy of *Reality Sandwiches*, "Talking about Pound, Libraries, Academia and Buddhist gossip."

In the spring of 1983, between our two formal meetings, I happened to mention, to two French professors of English who were teaching in our department that year, that Allen lived in Boulder. When they asked if I could introduce them to the poet, who enjoyed a tremendous reputation in Europe, I invited them all to lunch. Allen put on a bit of a show, and the rational French loved his outrageous yet congenial looniness. A hearty though vegetarian trencherman, Allen appreciated the food. Glancing at his watch, he mentioned that his friend Peter Orlovsky, in and out of confinement, had not been well lately and that he had to hurry home to make sure he was all right. I urged him to stay for dessert. My wife had baked, especially for him, a three-foot apple strudel that looked like a curled up, well-fed boa constrictor. Entering the kitchen to inspect, smell, and admire it, he announced, "Peter can wait!"

Before leaving, Allen presented my daughter with a signed-on-the-label 45-rpm Alekos record of him singing "Birdbrain" and "Sue Your Parents." He also signed a copy of *Howl*, drawing a daisy around the "o," and inscribed *Kaddish*, "Best wishes to a fellow fanatic writer."

Our second formal conversation, also in Boulder, took place two years later, in April 1985, while I was editing a book of essays, *The Legacy of D. H. Lawrence.* Allen had by then moved from Boulder to New York for some intellectual stimulation (notably absent in that village of frantic exercisers) and for closer contacts with editors and publishers. But he was still loyal to the troubled Naropa, taught during its spring week and summer session, and planned to make a Buddhist retreat in the fall. He had recently signed a six-book contract with Harper & Row, which seemed more lucrative than it actually was. *Time* had emphasized the marketing rather than literary significance, but he was getting only $25,000 a year. Nevertheless, the Harper deal and, later on, the million-dollar sale of his massive personal archive to Stanford had aroused jealousy rather than jubilation in the poetical ranks.

Ginsberg felt that Lawrence supplemented and reinforced the Williams lineage from Whitman. Lawrence criticized Whitman and rejected the body, but entered into a nongenital "heart relation" with other men. He was a model for specific detail, minute particulars, vivid facts, colorful images, spurts of perception; for awareness, abundance, profusion, dramatic movement, touches of sharp description, use of subjective facts about his own life. Ginsberg admired his rhythm and experiments with open form; his bold pioneering; his making new rules, especially in the animal and flower poems, in "Bat" and "The Ship of Death." Lawrence seemed wide open and abandoned, but he was also disciplined. He had a strong content and was a major innovator. Ginsberg, who shared Gary Snyder's sense of a mystical, Lawrencean revelation, described how Snyder "suddenly realized 'everything is alive'—the entire universe is alive. Every sentient being is alive, like myself."

When writing my life of Robert Frost, I asked Allen if he could tell me anything about him. On the back of an invitation to Snyder's reading in New York, he wrote that he'd never met Frost and that although he'd heard long-forgotten rumors, he didn't really know about

Frost's response to his poems. He liked some of Frost's poetry, first encountered through his father and in Louis Untermeyer's anthologies of the 1930s. He'd read about Frost's thirst for adulation, but had no firsthand knowledge of it. He did not recall discussing Frost with William Carlos Williams and, except for his now familiar "dark" texts, was blank about him. Predictably enough, Frost disliked Ginsberg's *Howl* and dismissed it by saying: "It's not very good—just a pouring out. Anyone can do it."

Allen often spoke of the difference between his mad public image, created by the media, and his real, serious self. Talking to him reminded me of Blake's *Songs of Innocence,* especially the closing quatrain of "Holy Thursday" about the multitudes of children:

> Now like a mighty wind they raise to heaven the voice of song,
> Or like harmonious thunderings the seats of heavens among.
> Beneath them sit the aged men, wise guardians of the poor;
> Then cherish pity, lest you drive an angel from your door.

Allen was at once an innocent child and a pity-filled old man.

II

In June 1981, the year before I first met Allen, I arrived in South Carolina to visit with James Dickey. I'd been investigating the death of Randall Jarrell and had just come from Chapel Hill, North Carolina, where he'd died. I'd interviewed the police, coroner, and doctors; found Jarrell's autopsy report; and concluded that he'd committed suicide. I was eager to talk to Dickey about Jarrell and find out what the inner circle knew about his death.

I'd prepared the way by sending him my life of Katherine Mansfield. In May 1981, in the second of his ten letters to me in the 1980s, he said that though he greatly admired her stories, he admired her fiery, bitchy, brittle character even more. He preferred to read her letters, or books *about* her, rather than her so-called artistic works.

I knew Dickey was a good athlete. I had suggested we play tennis and he replied that he'd be very pleased to take me on. He'd never played against Frost or Pound, but in the old days (he claimed), he could beat Roethke and Jarrell. Eager to plug into the poetic tennis tradition and beat the man who claimed to have beaten the highly touted Ted and Randall, I turned up ready for action. Jim, always intensely competitive, questioned me closely about my game and, sensing that I might beat him, declined the challenge.

Instead, he suggested a dart-blowing contest and snake hunt in the swamps. The dart competition took place, to my surprise, right in his living room, with the pine knots in the wood above the fireplace as targets. Inspired by the Amazonian headhunters, I held the long blowpipe, exhaled with cyclonic force, and hit the bull's-eye on my first shot. Jim was extremely irritated by my beginner's luck. We never went after the reptiles, but Jim promised, the following month, to have a snake hunt next time. He'd recently caught a six-foot water moccasin near his beach cottage on the Carolina coast, said there were a lot more down there, and promised to save one for me.

Jim had warned me that his second wife, Deborah, would give birth to their first child just before my arrival. When I got there, he showed me a local newspaper announcing the birth of chubby Bronwen with the headline "Deliverance" and a photo of the proud fifty-eight-year-old, baby-faced father holding up, as Ben Jonson had said, "his best piece of poetry." On my second visit, the following year, Bronwen toddled into the room and Jim heartily boomed out, "Luv ya, honey!" Startled, she burst into tears and fled. Large, and larger than life, the father of two grown sons seemed remote from his own little girl.

I was delighted when Jim offered to read in Colorado for a modest stipend as a special favor to me, and I looked forward to seeing him again. But when I suggested this to my colleagues in the English Department, they threw up their hands in horror. His previous visit (before my time) had been a complete disaster. Living up to his reputation as a wild poet, he'd been drunk, lecherous, and out of control—breaking up furniture, parties, and marriages.

At home and now married again (to a much younger wife), Jim was sober and fully in command, kind and extremely hospitable. He'd come up to Vanderbilt (he said) when Jarrell was still the prototype of the brilliant, promising poet. When he first met Jarrell in 1961, Jim was taken aback by his appearance, which did not match his high hopes. Looking much older than forty-seven, he was fragile and unathletic, with parchmenty eyelids. The writer Peter Taylor, a close friend of Jarrell, had told Dickey that a short time before his death, Jarrell had slashed his wrists and was being treated as an outpatient at a Chapel Hill hospital to rehabilitate the movement of his hands. Dickey believed that Jarrell's suicide was caused not by a failure of poetic power, but by his inability to achieve his impossible goals. He felt Jarrell had been a pampered literary genius, coddled by the top southern literary establishment—Ransom, Tate, and Warren—who acknowledged his great gifts very early in his career. Jarrell's ambition was to re-create the human sensibility. Tormented in middle age by his sense of failure, he became depressed and killed himself.

In September 1982, I published my essay "The Death of Randall Jarrell" in the *Virginia Quarterly Review*. Though Dickey had confirmed my views in conversation, he wrote that he'd been shocked by the realization that Jarrell had actually committed suicide. Randall was such a strong influence on his thought and response to things that he was horrified, even this late, to find that Jarrell had thrown away all that responsiveness, sensibility, and intelligence. He still found it too terrible to believe. Dickey praised Jarrell, but he ran down the rest of the manic poets. Though Randall was the best among them, they all failed at what they most desperately wanted to do—create significant and memorable poems. Berryman was so fake, affected, and mannered that his poetry seemed like a tasteless and self-deluding put-on. Schwartz, he felt, never wrote a single line of real poetry. Lowell seemed, in his later books, weaker than ever. And Elizabeth Bishop was, of course, no good at all. She was puffed up by Jarrell and Lowell but quickly evaporated when her clique expired. Though Dickey exaggerated, as always, he saw the weaknesses in Schwartz and Berryman. Though Lowell's late books show a decline from his earlier work, his reputation, like Bishop's, is now stronger than ever.

In December 1982, on the way to Key West to do research for a life of Hemingway, I stopped again to see Jim in South Carolina. At our second meeting he was very different and much less appealing. Strangely preoccupied and distracted, he exclaimed how glad he was to see me while remaining curiously disengaged from our conversation. I was struck by the contrast between his affable, generous, even courtly self in letters and on the phone and, when the veneer of southern politeness was stripped off, his aggressive boastfulness in person.

Dickey was highly critical of Hemingway and the mad poets, like Roethke and Jarrell, who had exposed their weakness by losing self-discipline and by succumbing to physical and mental illness. Jim blamed Hemingway for needing the harmful shock treatments and said he killed himself because he couldn't write any more. Dickey disliked Roethke and Jarrell for demanding special consideration, delicate handling, and sensitive care—for making excuses, in other words, for faults in their art.

On this occasion, like a cornered buccaneer, Jim angrily cut and slashed his way through the literary world. He said Pound was a swamp that one could sink in, and strongly disagreed when I praised Ginsberg's intellect. He scorned and pitied Mailer, dismissing him as a pathetic exhibitionist. He disliked poets in groups and sneered at politically biased poetry about the death of President Kennedy or the liberation of El Salvador. He didn't read contemporary poetry and knew of no younger poets he could praise. Ungenerous that day about everyone but himself, he seemed overcome by egoism.

He rather defensively remarked that he taught courses at the University of South Carolina in modern poetry and the teaching of poetry to give the bumpkins some sense of the poets he liked. One of his former students had made the film *Southern Comfort* (1981), a blatant rip-off of *Deliverance;* another had worked on movies with Bruce Lee and about aliens. He also mentioned his recent work: *Jericho* (1974), a coffee-table book about the old South for a Birmingham publisher; *Night Hurdling* (out in 1983), a book of essays; and reprints of the Anchor paperback editions of his poetry by Wesleyan University Press.

We then talked about *Deliverance* (1970). After writing the hill-climbing scene, he saw the possibility of a novel and worked out the rest from about 1962 to 1969, pushing hard to finish during the last three months. He loved the richly detailed novels of Dickens and Tolstoy, and was now working on a big World War II novel, part of which was published as "Cahill Is Blind" in the February 1976 issue of *Esquire.* (When the dreadfully titled *Alnilam* finally appeared in 1987, it was a complete flop.)

He conceded that Hemingway's "A Clean, Well-Lighted Place" was the best short story ever written, but felt that Hemingway was limited by a single style that he had mastered and never could surpass. He claimed that *Deliverance* was not influenced by Conrad, Faulkner, or Hemingway and, in another burst of hubris, insisted that it was better than *Heart of Darkness* or anything that Hemingway ever did.

Dickey wrote the screenplay of his novel, acted the sheriff and said he played the banjo in the film version, but didn't get credit for playing because he wasn't in the musicians' union. Inscribing his books with a graceful, loopy handwriting and a long, snakelike final *y* in *Jeffrey* and *Dickey,* he wrote in *Deliverance,* "these feathers, arrows and waters." In the screenplay of the novel (sent to me as promised), he emphasized the difference between what he originally wrote and what came out in the movie: "these rivers and arrows, in the *real* film."

Claiming he got a fee of half a million dollars for his film script of Jack London's *The Call of the Wild* (completed in 1976), Dickey said the television people paid well, but wanted control and unreasonable changes. Except for the screenplay of his forthcoming war novel, he'd never write for films again. In March 1989, two years after the novel appeared, he wrote me that he'd just finished writing the filmscript of *Alnilam*. If the director John Guillermin got the cast he wanted, they hoped to start filming the next fall. This movie, like so many Hollywood projects, has not yet been made.

Always encouraging about my own work, Jim seemed to like and admire biographies. He praised *A Fever at the Core* and my life of Wyndham Lewis, and offered to help me get jobs and grants. Keeping his word, in September 1982 he successfully recommended me for an American Council of Learned Societies award. He generously provided a blurb for my life of Hemingway, and when my biography of Edgar Poe appeared in 1992, he said: "Poe haunts the upper mind as an exalted and radiant justification of logic; and the unconscious as an obsession. Jeffrey Meyers shows us how, why and where these things go, and are going. God help us. But for Poe, we would never have known."

Our conversation had ranged over biography and its purpose, and as I was leaving he sweetly called me "an investigative reporter of the spirit." Then, realizing it was a bright phrase, he warned, "Don't let that one get away!" and urged me to write it down at once. In the last lines of his last letter to me, he told me to keep in close touch and said that I had his sincerest friendship and admiration. Though gratified by Jim's friendship and good opinion, I was troubled by what seemed a descent into blustering megalomania. His bravado appeared to mask, at least in the 1980s, a deep-rooted insecurity, which recalled a crucial passage in his appreciative essay on Roethke: "Why all this insistence on being the best, the acknowledged best, the *written-up* best? . . . And why the really appalling pettiness about other writers, like Lowell, who were not poets to him, but rivals merely? . . . His broad, boyish face had an expression of constant bewilderment and betrayal, a continuing agony of doubt."

Since I didn't return to Carolina and Jim was banned in Boulder, we didn't meet again. But we kept in touch by mail and phone. Creating a Roethkean persona of a poet who hung around with the tough guys and was pretty tough himself, he described putting down Helen Vendler, that book-burning Savonarola of criticism, when they both received honorary degrees at Kenyon College. He wrote that she'd knocked on his hotel-room door and, offering the garment, asked if this was his academic hood. Sweaty and unshaven, but still relaxed, gracious, and grave, he stood up and exclaimed that he *was* the academic hood.

In September 1993, after an appallingly obtuse review of his marvelous novel, *To the White Sea,* had appeared in the *New York Times Book Review,* Jim phoned to ask if I'd sharpen my pen and reply to it. I wrote, in a letter too severe to be published, that the "obscure reviewer admitted he neither understood the meaning of Dickey's lyrical, witty and dramatic novel nor how the hero achieved transcendence through a mystical identification with nature. The protagonist is not meant to be a pleasant fellow or a virtuous man. He's an expertly trained, self-reliant and necessarily ruthless survivor—like the heroes of *Heart of Darkness* and *The Call of the Wild.*"

If Allen recalled Blake's holy innocents, the broad and boyish-faced Jim seemed like Hopkins's boisterous, conflicted Felix Randal:

> Who have watched his mould of man, big-boned and
>   hardy-handsome
> Pining, pining, till time when reason rambled in it and
>   some
> Fatal four disorders, fleshed there, all contended?

2

Ed Dorn at Colorado

1929   born in Illinois
1955   graduates from Black Mountain College
1966   *The Shoshoneans*
1971   *By the Sound*
1968–75 *Gunslinger*
1977   begins teaching at University of Colorado
1999   dies in Denver

I

Ed Dorn and I were colleagues at the University of Colorado from 1977 to 1992. Despite two notable quarrels (we both had volatile tempers), we became good friends and spent a lot of time together. We dined and drank at each other's houses, visited mutual friends, went to parties, and attended the readings of writers who passed through town. We talked, for Ed—whose name means "thorn" in German—was a lively, contentious, and bitterly funny conversationalist. We talked about recent books and films, our current work, and the latest literary gossip.

But most of all we talked, endlessly and with malicious delight, about the ineptitude of the university administration (our sworn enemy) and about the envy and treachery, the idiocy and dullness of the colleagues that made up the English Department. The academic politics were intensely malicious because the issues were so trivial. Faculty who devoted their entire time to intrigue usually prevailed, for the serious writers soon gave up the fight to concentrate on their own work. Nevertheless, we wanted to record and analyze, as Flaubert had planned to do in his History of Human Stupidity, every instance of collegiate folly. Our criticism never achieved anything, of course, but it revealed the absurdity of the place, forged a common bond, and made us allies who had our own standards and opposed the endemic conformity.

When I arrived there in 1975, most of the recently hired younger faculty had had the stuffing kicked out of them when fired from their previous jobs. They professed eagerness to pursue higher research, but in reality were easing themselves into a permanent rest cure. An older colleague, wearily commenting on this phenomenon, said that coming to this university was like a bullet hitting water—you lost all momentum. The newcomers sucked up to the tenured, often comatose faculty, expressing gratitude in every weak smile and deferential nod. A younger man, eager for advancement, inscribed his book to one of the older wrecks, who'd never written anything, "To —, much admired, B. B." It wound up in the Salvation Army, where I bought it for a quarter. This agonizing tenure dance disgusted and disturbed me, but Dorn pretty much ignored it.

We were drawn together by our dedication to writing and respect for each other's work—though I was just beginning to hit my stride and reach a much wider audience, and Ed had clearly peaked with his book-length poem, *Gunslinger* (1968–75). Of his prose works, I particularly admired his book on Indians, *The Shoshoneans* (1966), and his novel, *By the Sound* (1971). When someone asked Ed, who wrote marginal works and published with small presses, if he was in touch with his readers, he replied, "Yes, I personally know all six of them!"

We also had very different attitudes toward the department, the university, and the town. I always thought that Boulder, on the divide between the Great Plains and the Rockies, had a complacent Midwestern mentality that strained to be Western. People constantly talked about buying a cabin in the mountains to "get away from it all." At 1,200 miles from the nearest coast, I was as far away as I ever wanted to be. I had come to Boulder after living for several years in Spain. Intensely dissatisfied with every aspect of Colorado, I never fitted in and never wanted to. Ambitious, eager to enhance my reputation as a critic and biographer, I was bitter about my slow promotion and low salary. I was desperately eager to find a job at a university with higher standards, more stimulating students and faculty. But the more I published, the more I dug myself in at Colorado, and as the universities contracted I never managed to find a better job.

By contrast, Ed had knocked around California, Washington, New Mexico, and Idaho, and for many years had just scraped by with occasional teaching stints. With a second family and two young children to support, he was glad to have finally found a secure and comparatively lucrative berth. Though well aware of the provinciality of Colorado, he liked living in the West, the source of much of his poetry, and had no desire to move.

Ed had already built a solid reputation. He was not interested in reviews of his poems, articles and books about his work, or his literary reputation in or out of Colorado. When I told him that an article on *Slinger* had appeared in the prestigious scholarly journal *American Literature,* he assumed it would be boring and showed no curiosity about it. In a letter of November 1982, he mentioned a forthcoming book, *Internal Resistances: The Poetry of Ed Dorn* (1985), and emphasized his ironic attitude with two words in quotation marks: "A 'good' note came in the other day with the news that UC Berkeley Press is going to publish a book of essays devoted to 'my' work. ¼ merit point looming on the western horizon, supposedly, since [in the wintry snow] we can't see much in that direction."

I felt, like Delmore Schwartz, "if you don't have a dog you must do your own barking," and tried to extract—through research money and grants that would free me to write—the maximum benefit from the university. Ed, though grateful for my efforts to make the department aware of his achievement and give him the proper reward, refused to exert himself on his own behalf. He was even content with a distant parking space while junior colleagues maneuvered themselves into high-status spaces next to the main office. Ed liked my iconoclasm, and I liked his indifference to reputation and material rewards.

Ed had a good deal of prestige but didn't get much out of the university. An effective public reader, he won his audience with witty, self-deprecating remarks that made his poems come alive. One of his star turns, in the tradition of William Carlos Williams, was the colorful, skillfully executed, and dramatically effective poem "Vaquero":

> The cowboy stands beneath
> a brick-orange moon. The top
> of his oblong head is blue, the sheath of his hips
> is too.
>
> In the dark brown night
> your delicate cowboy stands quite still.
> His plain hands are crossed.
> His wrists are embossed white.
>
> In the background night is a house,
> has a blue chimney top,
> Yi Yi the cowboy's eyes
> are blue. The top of the sky
> is too.

But he was usually—apart from clever remarks that went way over the students' heads—an unmotivated and unconcerned lecturer, swamped and depressed by an avalanche of hopelessly inept "creative" writing. Sometimes, in desperation, he'd simply fill up the fifty minutes by reading to the class from a printed book (not his own). He was a disaster as an exchange professor at Montpelier, where students expected lectures to prepare them for national exams on a fixed syllabus. Ed knew no French and spent most of his time exploring the countryside, apparently oblivious to the complaints about him. In class, Dorn could say, like the drunken Dylan Thomas, "Somebody's boring me—and I think it's me." Though I tried hard to wake the dead in my own classes, I rather admired Ed's offhand assumption that "if they're not good enough to understand what I'm trying to give them, why bother to teach them?"

The Creative Writing Program was split into two "experimental" but equally untalented factions. Both opposed traditional forms in poetry and prose, so that writers who attracted an audience with interesting stories and intelligible verse were resolutely excluded from visiting positions. The Fiction Collective, run by Ron Sukenick (Ed's archenemy), included Steve Katz, Bob Steiner, and Clarence Major. (Loyalties were somewhat strained when Major stole Steiner's wife.) The Idaho poet Richard Hugo, visiting Naropa one summer, pronounced the work of this group remarkable: they had perfected the art of being experimental without the aid of imagination. Sukenick, an effective operator, had a much higher salary than Dorn and had also convinced the university (always "striving for excellence," but never having a clue where to find it) to underwrite the group's publications, which no editor would publish and no reader touch. Students were occasionally forced to buy these books when they were assigned for a class. This gave new meaning to the idea of a "captive audience."

Dorn's sidekicks included cruder, earthier elements. Sidney Goldfarb, a good-natured oversized teddy bear, was notorious for never returning library books (sometimes recovered from his house, after a night raid by campus police, in disgraceful condition), for his gross eating habits, and for his "poem" about a fly landing on his ample ass. Peter Michelson, a specialist in pornography, was considered (though competition was keen) to be the dullest guy in the department. Dorn told me about attending the wedding of Peter's daughter, held in a shabby barn in a nearby town, where the bride was "kidnapped" by the groom's friends. Michelson passed around his cowboy hat and asked the guests for "ransom" money—an embarrassing local custom that made sure the caterer and the band got paid. Both groups of writers shamelessly courted graduate student disciples and trained them to replicate their inferior theories and techniques. It was, to paraphrase Wilde, the unspeakable in pursuit of the unteachable.

The best poet there, Bill Matthews, remained aloof. He was, with Dorn, the most sympathetic colleague among the self-promoters of the writing program. Sleepy-looking and puffy-faced, with a droopy mustache, he was an intelligent, ironic conversationalist. We played tennis together, but weren't close. Bill left Colorado for the University of Washington and I felt the loss of a colleague I could respect. He worked hard on behalf of other poets and died early, at the age of fifty-five, in 1997.

While I was teaching for a year at the University of Massachusetts, Ed kept me well informed—so I wouldn't feel too homesick—about the gossip, ennui, and minor tragedies in the department. In November 1982 he assured me that I was still in his thoughts: "You might have forgotten Boulder even exists but your absence is often noticed here. . . . [I was reading Emily Dickinson and] was in Amherst (in my mind) a lot in September and kept wondering how it was to be there on feet." He vividly described one of our leading alcoholics, now suffering from Parkinson's disease, as "cheerful as usual but getting around more like a man on wooden legs."

Worst of all, Ed wrote, were the endless but pointless department meetings: "Yesterday we discussed the fact that all we do is discuss. Then there was a long discussion about how to discuss stopping the discussion. But, mercifully, it was by that time, time to go." His wife, Jenny, added that as director that year, Ed "had to write a Report, justifying the Creative Writing Program. Jim Folsom [the Chairman] had to do a report for the whole English Dept. and the pressure exploded in a brain hemorrhage. He's still in the hospital trying to regain his left side which is totally paralyzed. Ed sat across from him at a committee meeting a few hours before his stroke and says he was absolutely beet red."

Jenny continued with one of our long-standing jokes—a friendly but highly exaggerated account of how I published more than all the rest of the department put together. ("Scribble, scribble, Mr. Gibbon" was often thrown my way.) "Ed seems to spend half his time at committees where your name is frequently mentioned," Jenny wrote, "like what publications has the dept. got on file for the year, where the answer is something like 50; ten from writing department, five from English and the rest Jeffrey Meyers."

An inexperienced bureaucrat, Ed seemed surprised that professors ran on at the mouth but couldn't focus their thoughts. The following month he brought me up to date with a satiric account of the tragicomic events: "At one point there was a debate, a long one, about whether the committee should find a way to limit the amount of time it spent talking. At that point I grew numb, like all over, and wondered if maybe Jim's stroke hadn't been a stroke of luck. And that's another thing: Jim insists he'll be teaching next semester but he can't walk yet." When another sickly colleague went into a diabetic coma during class, the students dozed on and didn't even notice the change.

At the end of each calendar year, the faculty had to fill out the notorious "yellow sheets," meant to record their intellectual achievements and used to determine salary increases, if any, for the following year. These sheets frequently recorded fictitious articles ("now being considered for publication") and absurd activities ("attended a 4-H meeting in Longmont"). Ed, on the budget committee that year, saw another vicious aspect of the department. My overflowing forms (extra pages needed) inspired a contrast between flatlands and mountains in one of Ed's pyrotechnical passages:

> Your letter created such disbelief around here for so long I stopped counting the times grown men wept at your vita Just For This Year. And their envy (laced with Ugandan disgust) made it seem like spring had jumped winter, the green was so pervasive. We didn't exactly play down the twisting-of-the-knife angle. Because for one thing, naturally, we were very pleased to hear such detail of such lowland adventures. All the more inciting because life along the upper barrens has been the same controlled hysteria you know as well as we.

The department's hostile attitude to my writing came to a head in February 1989, when friends nominated me for a distinguished professorship, a title that carried no extra money, but was meant to recognize published work. Several of these positions were now vacant, and I felt it would secure status not only for myself but also for the department and the subject of English. Colleagues opposed the nomination on the ground that I demanded too much of the graduate students and graded them too harshly. In answer Ed drew the battlelines and loyally supported me in a memorandum he read and distributed at a meeting: "I've heard it said that Professor Meyers is less than perfectly satisfying to graduate students. Leaving aside the prevailing sycophancy now

directed to that class and their 'student evaluations'—an oxymoron if
there ever was one—it has always been up to the student to find out
what they can use in the work and methods of so able a reseacher. . . .
I have always found his work trustworthy and useful, interesting and
enlightening."

We both loathed what Ed called the "disease" of French theory,
which had by then infected English departments across the country. He
agreed with Samuel Johnson, who condemned in his "Preface to Shakespeare" "those, who, being able to add nothing to truth, hope for emi-
nence from the heresies of paradox." Ed's memo concluded: "Meyers
maintains a cheerful disregard for those paranoias. He treats the world
with equanimity, and he treats the life [of his subject] with the respect it
deserves." Despite Ed's support, for he too was resented by the drones,
the department opposed the nomination ("better no one than him"),
and I did not get the distinguished professorship.

We also despised those student evaluations, a holdover from the
turbulent 1960s, where they served the healthy purpose of shaking up
the academy. They had now become a sort of market research tool that
told student-consumers how to get value for money: the highest grade
for the dumbest courses. Students graded teachers according to the
marks they had received, and faculty curried favor by lowering standards. For several years I refused to hand out these forms and suffered
financial penalties. Ed impressed me by taking a more radical step.
True to the sixties spirit, he made a happening out of it, burning his
evaluations in front of the class that had just filled them out.

II

Born in 1929 and ten years older than me, Ed was a tall, thin, square-
jawed, rough-looking man, with blue eyes, fair shaggy hair, and a
deeply grooved forehead and face. He had a slightly bulbous nose and
a smoker's husky voice. A striking oil portrait of himself, sometimes
used to announce his readings, hung on the wall and seemed to confirm
his identity. Like Boulder itself, Ed, who came from Illinois, masquer-
aded as a Westerner. He wore a wide-brimmed Stetson, leather vest,
and cowboy boots that seemed to go with his long, ruggedly handsome
face.

His personality was strongly marked by the events of his early life.
A bastard, he never knew his father, who abandoned his son before he
was born. I don't think Ed ever forgave either parent for this rocky start
in life, and he had a deep-rooted resentment about his emotional de-

privation and early poverty in the prairie town of Villa Grove. He disliked upper-class people, elegant clothes, fine manners, formal speech, and anything self-consciously literary. Guarded and defensive, except when expressing anger, Ed was a loner. He rarely revealed his deepest feelings, the more tender and sensitive side of his nature, and it was hard to break through his reserve and get close to him. He never mentioned his mother, his first wife, or his grown children. So I was surprised in December 1982 when he matter-of-factly wrote: "My mother is probably going to die soon—heart failure. I'm going to take my son, who is coming out from Boston the 31st to see her in the first week [of] January—to Illinois." When his mother died in one of the following winters and he couldn't get a cheap plane ticket at the last moment, he set out in his old wreck of a car and drove to her funeral through a thousand miles of snowstorms.

Compared to all the Ph.D.'s in the department, Ed—with a year at the University of Illinois and some patchy courses at the eccentric Black Mountain College—was poorly educated. He uncritically revered his poetic masters—Pound, Charles Olson, Robert Creeley, and the obscure geographer Carl Sauer. Unfamiliar, for example, with John Donne, he called me up to ask what books to read and how to teach him. He covered the large gaps in his knowledge, his ignorance of things an English professor would normally know, with dogmatic assertions. He liked to argue, to be provocative and outrageous, but he was often narrow-minded and inflexible.

Ed had a satiric outlook. His rebarbative comments were accompanied by a deep, loud "ha-ha-ha" belly laugh that often anticipated the point of his caustic thrust. He liked to sprinkle his speech with a few Spanish words—*libros, mucho, nada, mundo*—as if to mock the multicultural mania. When I missed a deadly lecture that he, as a member of a search committee, was required to attend, he treated me to a hilarious imitation of the feminist candidate's speech. With raised, swaying arms and fingers clicking imaginary castanets, he did a mock-Spanish dance to show how she indicated the fatuous (and then-fashionable) quotation marks around her key words.

Another prime target was John Martin, the publisher of Black Sparrow Press. I maintained that Martin produced serious, well-designed books and ran a profitable business. Ed, who resented Martin's luxurious house and swimming pool, mocked his tight-assed Mormon mentality and notorious reluctance, even unwillingness, to pay his authors. He took delight in the sexual scandals and fuzzy-minded gullibility of the local Buddhists, and was hilarious and scathing about one of the dimmer lights among the creative writers. A purveyor of "sensitive" (arms raised for "castanets") sentimental tripe about her East Indian childhood, she was either on leave or, when in town, too "indisposed" to do anything but collect her paycheck.

Ed didn't care about money and thought a poet, as befitted that high calling, should live austerely, unencumbered by material possessions. A child of the Depression, he had a deep distrust of the stock market and financial investments, and was suspicious of unearned income. He didn't understand the advantages of owning property or taking a tax deduction for a mortgage, and always refused to buy his own home. (After I'd left Boulder, he finally bought a house in Denver.) Instead— like a tenant farmer on the old plantation—he lived in a humble dwelling opposite his landlord's high-columned mansion on Mapleton Avenue, the classiest street in town.

Jenny proudly wrote, when I was away in Amherst, that Ed "built the coalshed in the back into a great little cabin, all insulated and snug and just big enough for a bed and a desk. Now when people come a-visiting at the wrong time, he doesn't have to know about it, he's safely hidden away in the back yard." When I saw the place myself, the spartan shack looked like an upended coffin, more a preparation for the grave than a writer's retreat.

Always defiant and anarchistic, Ed grew his own marijuana, which I didn't notice—as I didn't smoke myself—until one Sunday afternoon. While having drinks in his garden, we heard a bang and some shouting in the street. Suddenly, a couple of cops vaulted the fence at the bottom of the garden and came tearing up toward us. They were chasing a young man who'd stolen a car, crashed it, and run off. Jenny stood up, spread her skirt, and danced in front of the potted plants around the kitchen door. Both Dorns were nervous, but the police were too intent on the chase to inspect the greenery.

Ed's transportation matched his residence. A gigantic old gas-guzzler, which needed nearly two parking spaces, was succeeded by a rattling canvas-and-plastic–topped Jeep, which was paralyzingly cold during the long harsh winters. His proletarian stance, however, was offset by a few quirky interests. Though he had nothing in common with the duffers in green trousers and polyester shirts, he liked to play golf. He and Jenny played the occasional game of ragged tennis. And, always light on his feet and wanting to please Jenny, he astonished me by taking tango lessons—in Boulder! He'd play the tango tapes in the car and, listening to the beat as if still dancing, would switch his hands on the steering wheel and comically shift his head from side to side.

Both Ed and I had spent a lot of time in England, were loyal Anglo-philes, and had English wives who were skillful editors and taught the freshman composition course. We both devoured his copies of the *Manchester Guardian Weekly*. Knowing my wife was nostalgic for London, he gave her a travel poster that she'd admired on his wall—a view of the Thames adorned with a famous quote by Samuel Johnson. Ed cunningly changed it to read, "When a *woman* is tired of London, *she* is tired of life," and charmingly suggested the words were written for her. We sometimes talked about the ideal place to live. I preferred Hampstead, while Ed, who'd taught at the University of Essex from 1965 to 1970, thought that Newmarket, with its open green racecourse, would be best.

While at Essex, he'd incurred the wrath of his moralistic mentor, the poet-critic Donald Davie, by leaving his wife Helene and two children to marry his much younger student, Jennifer Dunbar. Ed and Jenny had mixed emotions about this delightful but discreditable episode, and didn't like to talk about it. Jenny came from an unusual family. Her mother was Russian; her father had worked in films (including *The Third Man*) and given Jenny an interest in the subject, which she studied and taught. She had a twin sister, and her brother had been married to the pop singer Marianne Faithfull.

Lively, sympathetic, and sexy, Jenny had a tiny waist and knockout figure, a fine-boned face and extraordinary green eyes. She also had a gravelly voice, a smoker's cough, and a haggard look. A good hostess, she liked to cook hearty stews and casseroles. She started but never finished a confusing number of projects, including a book on an American rock singer who became a star in East Germany and died in mysterious circumstances in East Berlin.

Their children, Kid and Maya (who wanted to be a folksinger), were blond, good-looking, wide eyed, and distinctly unacademic. When my wife mentioned that she was tutoring a hairy, muscular Mexican boy, several years older than the other students in his class at the junior high, Kid, a skinny thirteen-year-old, awed by the unlikely conjunction, exclaimed: "*You* know José? He's *tough!*"

III

One never knew which way Ed—intensely emotional and wildly inconsistent—would jump during an argument. During the dreary Reagan decade, we got into heated disputes about the Falklands War (1982) and the invasion of Grenada (1983). As the British fleet slowly steamed to the wintry South Atlantic, the anarchistic Ed was suddenly pro-Thatcher, jingoistically British, and hell-bent on blasting the Argies off the barren rocks. The following year, when the Americans landed on Grenada, Ed reverted to form, condemned U.S. aggression, and distributed his own bumper sticker that read, "PRINT THE INVASION MONEY!" After George Bush was elected, Ed, irreverent as ever, installed a light-switch panel that featured the new president. His pink penis could be flicked up and down to turn the living room light on and off.

In December 1988, when the London *Observer* commissioned him to write a piece on the Tenth Havana Film Festival, he had another opportunity to express his political views. He described the Cuban atmosphere and the films he saw, and concluded with a vivid glimpse of Fidel himself. Ignoring Fidel's oppressive rule, he mentioned that Batista's Ministry of Justice building was "still worth a shudder from the outside." Admitting that the hotel rooms "lacked showers, TVs, and balconies but had plenty of cockroaches," he defended the Castro regime and emphasized the positive achievements of Communist rule: "an infant mortality rate comparable to the Scandinavians', universal health care, the establishment of literacy, enough to eat for the first time in their history."

Fidel's continuous movement during his early years in power, Ed jokingly wrote, "must have been the original idea for the MX missile system." When the great dictator unexpectedly appeared at the film festival, "he was wearing a general's uniform with a little gold braid and a red star. He was accompanied by only three or four bodyguards who were as pressed as he was by the surge. He stayed with the people, touching hands over the heads of those closest to him, and speaking earnestly and affably with those nearest. He seemed at ease with all this"—and so did Ed.

IV

By the time he arrived in Boulder, Ed went in for the aggressive dogmatism that characterized his *Interviews* and *Abhorrences,* and wrote verse that was as sloppy and self-indulgent as "Vaquero" and *Gunslinger* were artful and accomplished. Instead of concentrating hard on his own work, he spent most of his time (and a great deal of Jenny's) bringing out the bottom-of-the-drawer stuff of Michelson, Goldfarb, and "Dobro" Dick Dillof, a self-styled cowboy poet in Montana. All this found a home in Ed's tacky but beloved newspaper *Rolling Stock.*

Its motto—"If It Moves Print It"—mocked the *New York Times'* "All the News That's Fit to Print" and suggested its unfocused, shotgun effect (it even had a golf column). Ed got into hot water in the second number with Goldfarb's critique of Israeli policy in Lebanon, entitled "Kike to Kike." No wonder Jenny wrote, around that time: "Financial/business side of this enterprise is getting to be depressing. . . . We're non-profit and going under." They eventually wised up and, following Sukenick's hat-in-hand lead, managed to persuade the university to support their project.

At Ed's request I contributed a serious piece to *Rolling Stock*—a comparison of Robert Louis Stevenson and D. H. Lawrence—as well as two lighter ones: a satire on fanatical T. E. Lawrence collectors and a mildly amusing parody for the imitation-Hemingway contest. This last piece caused a quarrel by mail when I was spending a year in England and a temporary cooling of our friendship when I returned to Colorado.

Always terribly casual about the way he ran the paper—the writing was sloppy and it never came out on time—Ed informed me that the printer had trouble setting this last piece, "at which point we frankly abandoned it. I hope you will understand & not mind that." After throwing out the work he had asked for and accepted (and for which he paid nothing), he then requested I write something else: "What we'd like from you but almost don't dare ask is a 'London Diary' w/ highlites of your impressions, visitations, acrimonies & most shaded thoughts, enthusiasms (if any). In other words, the Murdochs & Boondocks of the capital of the olde empire."

In fact, I was rather fond of this piece, minded very much, and shot back a furious reply. This storm in a teacup revealed contrasting attitudes to our work. I wanted to publish everything I wrote. Ed, more casual, didn't share this view, and my anger surprised him. For him, the important thing was the newspaper. He disclaimed editorial responsibility but, soothing my anger, agreed to publish it soon: "Why don't you lighten up? You're forcing me to suspect something psychological is going on. Treacherous applied to me has practically no meaning, and I never told anybody I was 'responsible.' The point is we both do miss the periodic sessions we had with you and Val. Strong talk is an even rarer commodity around here since y'all been gone."

Stimulated by our talks and genuinely fond of one another, despite occasional contention, we soon returned to our dinners and to blistering attacks on the department. His friendly feelings toward me, and comments on his books, he recorded in my copies of his works:

The Shoshoneans: "For Jeffrey, amigo in the short cactus country."
From Gloucester Out: "For Jeffrey Meyers, Biographer Maximus."
Slinger: "For J. Meyers. ~~From~~ To Bullslinger from Gunslinger."
Streeter, *A Bibliography of Ed Dorn:* "T. B." [Terrible Book].
Some Business Recently Transacted in the White World: "Not so
    recently now, but I hope still <u>there</u>."
Views: "Here's hoping there's still a little news in the views."

V

About twice a year Ed and I would load the car with food and drink—
so we'd be sure to have them when we ascended 12,000 feet to Rollins-
ville—and make a congenial visit to the experimental filmmaker Stan
Brakhage. We'd spot the old car that housed the goats in the front yard
and pile into the roughly constructed, eccentrically bohemian house,
full of children and pet snakes, which sat in a clearing in the midst of
huge pines. Stan—adopted when three weeks old from a home for un-
wed mothers—had had a nervous breakdown that forced him to drop
out of Dartmouth after three months. He was a bearded, pear-shaped
man, his eyes so deep-set that he looked almost blind. Though refresh-
ingly enthusiastic and intransigently avant-garde in his own work
(comparing the great traditional films to comic books), he had old-
fashioned literary taste and admired the obsolete biographies of Emil
Ludwig. After commuting for years to teach a film course at the Art Institute in Chicago, Stan finally landed a half-time job at the University
of Colorado.

We'd cram into his cigarette- and wood smoke–filled private theater, drink the wine and whiskey that were doubly powerful at high
altitudes, and watch Stan's highly prized, migraine-making films: his
wife in labor with their first child, waves breaking endlessly against
some rocks, fluffy towels falling into a heap—the kind of soft focus,
very slow slow motion he had pioneered. Stan showed us his work in
progress—the hand-painted frame-by-frame abstracts he began to do,
slowly and with infinite care—the most tedious and perplexing film I'd
ever seen. He and Ed, it seemed, were determined to offer the world
what it needed and clearly didn't want. On the way down the mountain I'd open the window to wake myself with an icy blast, clutch the
steering wheel, and try to keep the car from hitting a deer or sliding off
the road into the canyon.

Ed and Jenny came to my fiftieth birthday celebration (his birthday
was the day after mine), and to various dinners at my house to meet

scholarly friends like Denis Donoghue and Donald Greene. Donald, frail and elderly at this point, puffing on a chain of cigarettes and downing one drink after another, had a minor stroke and collapsed at the dinner table (I just managed to catch him before he hit the floor). When Don seemed near death, Ed swore he'd stop smoking—and kept his word.

Ed sometimes invited me to dinners for visiting writers. When he had nothing in common with the guests, the atmosphere got prickly despite the flow of drink. Kay Boyle—tall, gangly, and unattractive—was extremely pleased with herself and hated Hemingway. After her friend Robert McAlmon had spread malicious rumors that Hemingway was a homosexual, Papa gave him a well-deserved punch on the nose. Boyle, still indignant after fifty years, held me—as Hemingway's biographer—responsible. On another occasion the red-faced, beaky-nosed John Ashbery, who affected a prissy, supercilious manner, confided he'd slept with the elderly Auden "to see what it was like" (not too great). When asked why he'd used the Parmigianino painting "Self-Portrait in a Convex Mirror," he evasively replied, "Because the boy was cute."

Ed and I liked to go to public readings so we could check out the traveling talent and find fault with the show. In each case my impression of the writer was stronger than the memory of what he actually said. The handsome, refined novelist Giorgio Bassani (lacking only a monocle and a cane) was worth seeing, we thought, for his *elegantissimo* white linen suit, perforated gloves, and fine leather briefcase. With a good grasp of English but a bewildering pronunciation (he said "tree-tree" for "territory"), he left the audience more confused than if he'd spoken in Italian.

Manuel Puig was a thin, shy, Argentine homosexual, forced into exile by the military regime. Puig was speaking to me in Spanish at a party before his reading when a monolingual Chicana "poet" came up and we were obliged, for her sake, to switch into English. Puig's reading, to an enormous audience that reflected his popular success, was as weak and attenuated as he was. Some bad shrimp I had eaten at the party made me turn green and rush out to throw up outside the building.

The prim, narrow-lipped, and surprisingly uptight William Burroughs looked more like a druggist than a druggee. Sinister and skeletal, he was flanked by two rough-trade bodyguards. As a writing technique, he seriously recommended cutting individual words out of magazines, throwing a handful of them into the air and typing them up as they randomly fell on the floor. Though manifestly absurd, we thought the results of this method would be no worse than the more traditional efforts of our students.

Jorge Luis Borges—with the glazed, vacant look of the blind—was led around by his keeper and would-be biographer. Frail, with long upper lip and strangely tilted nose, Borges greeted people like an old-world diplomat as they joined a long receiving line to ask him questions. The following day, as remote as ever at a graduate seminar in Spanish, Borges tried hard to make his meaning understood. But the queries about his enigmatic work were as confusing as his cryptic, oracular answers.

When I was abroad, Ed kept me abreast of the local absurdities. After Creeley's reading, he wrote, the greedy audience "descended on the wine and cheese with the efficiency of the gulls who saved the Mormon crops from the locusts in 1851 or thereabouts." Another reading, by my replacement from Amherst, "dull enough to make you slit your wrists," he compared to the budget committee meeting: "Again, grown men were crying but this time there was nothing to envy. Actually, I rather, at times, enjoyed the pain. . . . The whole thing was like Page [auditorium] actually looks: a cheap funeral parlor trying to pass."

Just before I left teaching and Boulder in 1992 to write full-time and live in Berkeley, I went to my last Dorn party, where Ed was at his worst. Slightly drunk, he pontificated in front of his adoring but ignorant disciples, who literally and figuratively sat at his feet. Angrily defending Pound, denying the overwhelming evidence of the *Cantos* and the published wartime broadcasts, he argued that the poet had never been anti-Semitic. His blindness about Pound's bigotry, which had done great harm during the war when Italian Jews were in mortal danger, had its roots in Ed's impoverished provincial background. Since this sort of argument is common in academic circles (the late Eloise Hay, an Eliot scholar, once told me that "only kikes think Eliot was anti-Semitic") and the students believed what he said, I countered Ed's assertions and we got into a shouting match. When he dug in his heels and refused to accept the factual evidence, I left his party and never saw him again.

The following year, when tempers had cooled and I was settled in Berkeley, Jenny sent a friendly letter: "We think of you both quite often, and miss you not being around. It's hard to live in this town without someone to share notes with. . . . Ed feels the same way and says it's rare now for him to have an intelligent conversation."

In the spring of 1998 Ed's friend Tom Clark told me Ed was seriously ill and I phoned to find out how he was. He'd suffered stomach pain, was told he had an ulcer, and had wasted precious time taking useless medication. In April 1997 a CAT scan revealed that he actually had pancreatic cancer. Radical surgery showed that the malignancy had spread to other organs and was inoperable. So he was sewn up and given three different kinds of treatment. Experimental pills and bi-weekly chemotherapy had not worked, and he was now taking weekly drugs with powerful side effects, which inhibited the slow-growing but inexorable tumor. His attitude had evolved from denial and rage to a determined effort to fight the disease and finish his work.

It had been a grim year for Ed. His weight dropped from 170 to 135 pounds and, though he still had energy, he lacked strength. The prognosis "by the book" was bad, and the doctors had made no predictions, but it was clear that he was surviving on borrowed time. Trying to live the life that remained to the fullest, he gave a poetry reading in Berkeley in November 1997 and the following month took his family on holiday to Ochos Rios in Jamaica. They enjoyed the jewel-like scenery and fine Botanical Garden, and found the people—despite the horror stories about Kingston—pleasant, upbeat, and lighthearted. Despite his grave illness, Ed was determined to teach a final semester in the fall of 1998. He said he needed the money. But it was even more important, I think, to be around people, connect with his students, and get a shot of admiration that could now work better than any medicine.

Characteristically, Ed was not afraid to examine his illness, recording in his notebooks the effects on him of the various drugs, including painkillers and antidepressants, and writing a bitterly punning work called "Chemo-Sabe." He was working on a long poem, "High Plains," and, with his old collaborator Gordon Brotherston, on some old and new translations of Latin American poets, to be handsomely published by North Atlantic Books in Berkeley. He spoke more slowly and quietly than usual. But—brave, stoical, and dignified, despite the midnight agonies—he kept his fighting spirit.

3

Arthur Miller

1915	born in New York City
1938	graduates from University of Michigan
1947	*All My Sons*
1949	*Death of a Salesman*
1953	*The Crucible*
1956–61	marriage to Marilyn Monroe
1962	marries Inge Morath
1987	*Timebends*
	now lives in Connecticut

I

In the 1970s I wrote two literary biographies: one on Katherine Mansfield, a short story writer from New Zealand who died early at the peak of her career; the other on Wyndham Lewis, an original novelist, great painter, and incurable outsider who died blind and neglected in 1957. As I began to consider a new subject, my biographer's antennae quivered at the thought of Arthur Miller. His opposition to the infamous House Un-American Activities Committee (HUAC) in the 1950s had earned him lasting political prestige. His plays were a staple of the American theater repertory, and he'd also written classic film scripts of his own work. Though his normal, commonsensical, intellectual life rarely made headlines, in the late 1950s he had been married to Marilyn Monroe, a conjunction that made heads spin at the time and now seemed the stuff of myth. I was full of respect for him, and curiosity as well.

In September 1980 I wrote to sound him out. I couldn't help noting in my letter the similarities between his early life and mine. We both came from Jewish families, grew up in New York, had a father in the coat business, were adored by our mothers (who slept late while the maid served breakfast), were taught by Irish spinsters in public schools, rebelled against piano lessons and Hebrew school, and graduated from the University of Michigan.

Not surprisingly, Miller didn't want to be distracted from his current work by contemplating the shape and pattern of his entire life. He did not want a sleuth to comb through his private papers for unwelcome revelations. Nor did he want to give away material and ideas he still might use in his own writing. But he replied courteously and, as I learned to expect, modestly: "I would be loath to begin a project such as you suggest for several reasons. I am really writing more now than ever in my life and I don't want to interrupt. I've never kept anything like an orderly file of all my correspondence, most of which, in any case, is hardly worth reading. And finally, I guess, I don't think I'm all that fascinating"—though he was about to write his own autobiography.

This last remark might seem disingenuous. Miller's life, lived at the center of American cultural history, had been a starring role, not a walk-on part. But he was making a distinction between the complex external events and his straightforward inner character. As an enormously successful playwright, he must have had extraordinary ambition and drive, been innovative, even rebellious. He must have made personal sacrifices and taken infinite pains. Did he, in fact, retain the human sympathy and self-respect that had sparked his imagination and informed his greatest work? Was there a modest man, an ego under control, inside his creative personality? If so, he must be quite different, I thought, from the selfish, driven, often tragic artist that lies at the heart of most literary biographies. This distinction made him all the more interesting to me.

My letter began our relationship. He asked me to send him my book on Mansfield, and read it attentively. "Though I usually distrust biographies," he wrote, "to the point of avoiding them whenever possible, yours I believed. . . . She is one of those tragic persons launched on a short trajectory, the self-consuming rocket." He invited me to visit him in Connecticut, and in June 1981 I made the first of nine visits, extending over the next seventeen years.

Arthur had bought this rustic house in 1956, a retreat from Manhattan and the theater, but close enough to New York to keep an eye on the city. Down a country lane, surrounded by forty acres of woods and meadows, it was set on a rise above a swimming pond. He came out to meet us, six feet tall, as straight-backed as a soldier, his white hair crowning his tanned bald head and his Jeffersonian face, familiar from many press photographs. He was as unpretentious as his house, a comfortable place with oriental rugs on the floor, colorful sofas, books overflowing the bookcases and scattered around the rooms. He had a carpentry workshop and separate studios for himself and his wife, the photographer Inge Morath. As we walked through the grounds, he pointed out the plants and vegetables in their garden, and moths laying eggs in the grass.

Arthur was a powerful physical presence. I was aware of his large capable hands, his denim workshirt, his shorts and muscular legs, his bare feet in moccasins. He mowed the huge lawn himself, replaced the cement on the patio, and made his own furniture. He was proud of his new custom-built Finnish woodstove, made of soapstone; he had been using the leftover material to carve building blocks and had assembled them to look like miniature stage sets and a modern city filled with skyscrapers. He cut a lot of wood and for him trees had distinctive characters: he showed me his "wolf-tree," which dominated and devoured all the other trees around it. It had seeds that flourished only if they drifted far away.

Though he tried to "hide out" in Connecticut, many people came to see him, and he had some illustrious neighbors: Alexander Calder, Richard Widmark, Dustin Hoffman, Philip Roth, and William Styron (on whose court Arthur played tennis). Norman Mailer had once lived nearby. In this quiet, seemingly remote place he seemed more a countryman than a sophisticated New Yorker. (In 1984, when Arthur was in China, a fire from a defective oil burner destroyed the main house, along with his books and personal possessions. Fortunately, his studio was unharmed and his papers were safe. His insurance was excellent and, though it took six months to restore everything, the new house was much better than the old one. He called it "one of the best fires I ever had.")

He probably earns more money from books and plays than any other serious writer. His plays, produced all over the world, are staged more frequently than those of any other dramatist save Shakespeare. (Though his agents, he told me, were lucky to collect half of what was owed in Asia and Africa, in Europe and South America he did well. He sometimes has five plays on in England in one year.) He had a new Mercedes and a Rabbit convertible in the garage, and we talked about driving into Manhattan. He was pleased to have found a cheap place to park, but liked it even more when he was chauffeured into town for a premiere and could sleep on the way back. He had one of the new wireless phones, run off a battery, which he carried around while he did the chores, and was delighted by the convenience when it rang and actually worked.

Rich he must be, but he didn't act rich, didn't seem in the least acquisitive or flashy. Fame, too, had a price. Ruefully, he told me his niceguy reputation inspired ten to twenty letters a week from strangers asking for, even demanding, large sums of money for all kinds of needs —school tuition and medical expenses. Though his face is not so famous that he stands out in the crowd, he had recently been stopped in the street in New York by a man who recognized him and insisted that Arthur help him publicize a new theory about light refraction. The light in the man's own pale gray eyes was disquieting, and Arthur had gotten rid of him with difficulty.

The table was set for lunch out in the sunshine, and as we sat down Inge appeared, in a hurry to drive across the countryside to New Haven. She was taking a course in Chinese at Yale in preparation for their long trip—she to take photographs, he to direct *Death of a Salesman* in Beijing. Thin, birdlike, and dynamic, Inge welcomed us warmly, said goodbye to "Arr-toor," and departed in a cloud of energy. We had smoked salmon, a rich salad, and homemade rye bread. Arthur's Austrian mother-in-law, round, placid, and charming, had baked a superb strudel.

Sitting across the table, Arthur looked strong and handsome. He'd injured his knee in a youthful football game and been rejected by the army in World War II. Recently, he'd fallen off a ladder and broken his ankle. (With it still in a cast he'd sailed up the Nile in Sadruddin Khan's yacht to see the Pharaonic monuments.) Just before a trip to South America, a tear in his retina almost blinded him. During a seven-hour emergency operation, performed the next day, the surgeon took the eyeball out of the socket and fastened a "buckle" around it to keep the tear from spreading. Though Arthur continued to be bothered by mist in his distant vision and had to rest his eyes in the afternoon, the operation saved his sight and gave him 20/20 vision with glasses. Apart from his ankle and his eyes, he was in remarkably good shape for a man of sixty-six.

Tilting back his chair, pushing back his glasses, and jutting out his lower jaw as he talked, Arthur was warm, friendly, even paternal. At ease with himself, if not with the world—for he could be surprisingly severe—he made me feel immediately at ease, as if I had known him forever. It was hard to imagine him ever playing the temperamental artist or pompous great man. A social being, who seemed to like visitors, he spoke genially and naturally about everything, though it was tacitly understood that I would not interrogate him. I didn't associate such repose with writers. His plays dramatized universal themes, common to all men in all languages: unconscious fears, domestic and political conflicts. His reputation was secure; he showed no arrogance. He was actively engaged in writing and getting his new plays produced, yet he didn't seem competitive. He talked all afternoon, listened attentively, and asked me to come back on my next trip east.

II

On my second visit we exchanged life stories, as people getting to know each other do, and Arthur talked more extensively about his past and present. His father, he said, had been barely literate but prosperous, his mother a high school graduate. They had lived comfortably in Manhattan, with servants and a chauffeur. When Arthur was fourteen his father lost everything in the Wall Street Crash, and never recovered his business or his wealth. He moved the family to Brooklyn and, cushioned by his remaining jewels and property, drifted slowly into poverty. This was the crucial experience of Arthur's life—the Depression, the ugly side of capitalism made manifest—which devastated the lives of his family and friends, but also inspired his poignant portrayal of Willy Loman. For the rest of his life he would sympathize with those who were exploited and then found themselves used up and discarded. He told me the recent story of a local Connecticut tractor agent he knew who had been in business for forty-six years and lost his contract with the manufacturer when his sales declined. Arthur and Richard Widmark had written a letter of protest to the company, but it had made no difference.

Arthur married for the first time in 1940, Mary Slattery, a lapsed Catholic classmate at the University of Michigan who became a school psychologist. In 1956 they had a bitter separation, and he had not seen her for twenty years. Reflecting on the houses he had lived in (so important to a writer, whose home is his workshop), he told me that after his first success in the theater he had bought a Brooklyn Heights brownstone for $32,000 and lived there with his wife in the early 1950s. She had recently sold it for $650,000.

He bought the present Connecticut house, his second, when he married Marilyn Monroe. I pictured him in my mind's eye in all the photographs of the period, when the flashbulbs popped incessantly and Arthur Miller's face appeared next to Marilyn's in *Picture Post* and *Photoplay*. At forty-one, in the prime of his life and achievement, he was thinner then, tense and bespectacled. He didn't seem to go with the fluffy, artificial, lipsticked time bomb he had married. I thought of the photos of the group on location for *The Misfits* in the Nevada desert —Clark Gable, Montgomery Clift, Monroe, all doomed to die within the year—and Arthur, watching his screenplay develop as Monroe unraveled. Sitting in the lush quiet of the garden, I said surely this place must have made Marilyn happy. "Nothing could make Marilyn happy for very long," he flatly observed.

He spent so much on her treatment that he had to sell his literary manuscripts to the University of Texas. "Wasn't she rich, couldn't she pay for her own doctors?" I asked. He explained that, on the contrary, she was broke. She'd signed a seven-year contract with Fox that kept her on the same low salary after she became famous and earned them a fortune. Her photographer, Milton Greene, had formed a joint corporation with her, literally owning 49 percent of her. Arthur prevented him from getting majority control, but eventually Marilyn had to pay $100,000 to get rid of him.

From talk of Marilyn it was a short step to Norman Mailer, Arthur's bête noire, and to all the books about Marilyn "by trashy writers who never took her seriously." I then realized why Arthur was so sceptical about biography. He was particularly severe about his once close friend and collaborator Norman Rosten, who wrote the screenplay for *A View from the Bridge*, and called his book on Marilyn "superficial, vulgar, and self-justificatory." (Rosten had begun his career by winning a Yale Younger Poets prize, but he never fulfilled his promise.) Mailer's bizarre *Marilyn* (1975), a fantastical fiction masquerading as biography, claimed that Miller lived off her earnings, though Mailer could easily have found out that the reverse was true. Mailer invented witty and satiric remarks, directed against Miller, and put them into Marilyn's mouth. Arthur considered suing him, but finally decided that doing so would only help promote the book. At this point he was more disgusted than angry.

Arthur also thought the theory that the Kennedys had Marilyn murdered was absurd. She was probably sexually involved with them, but they were unlikely to have told her anything incriminating. In any case, she was loyal and they had no reason to kill her. As for Arthur's own relationship with Marilyn, which he did not talk about, I had the feeling that his happiness must have been brief, and that he'd spent most of his time trying to help this talented, wounded woman. Abused by so many men on her way to the top, she'd had several abortions and miscarriages. When they met she was suffering from depression and addicted to prescription drugs. The odds were against them, the decision to marry her an impulsive gamble for someone as self-controlled and self-respecting as Arthur Miller.

Inge Morath, by contrast, was and is eminently sane, strong, capable, and self-reliant. Always warm and welcoming—not the self-important dragon-guardian, like some literary wives—she is a cultured and sophisticated European intellectual, critical and alert. Her career and travels mesh with Arthur's, and she admires his work without lionizing him.

On a later visit I mentioned that the publisher of my Hemingway biography had asked for an author's photograph. Inge responded immediately and enthusiastically. She brought out several cameras, told Arthur to continue our conversation so we'd have more natural expressions, and took several rolls of pictures. Later on, she let me use the best photo for a small fee. We walked over to her studio, once an old silo, now with a darkroom and space for layout and storage. It was filled with her magnificent shots of Picasso, Cocteau, Neruda, Kosinski, and Janet Flanner.

Arthur has two children from his first marriage and one from his third. His son, Robert (born in 1947), who lived in California and worked in television, was a driving force in the recent movie of *The Crucible*. To raise money for this project, Arthur had sold in advance the rights to show the film on network television and HBO. Sixty directors, including Arthur Penn, had turned the film down because it had to be made in thirty days and none of them thought it could be done. Arthur's agent, Sam Cohn of International Creative Management (ICM), reputedly the best in the business, had grave doubts they'd ever sell such a serious work in the age of "bang-bang" films. Finally, Robert asked if he could have the rights for six months. Within a few weeks, he sold it to Twentieth Century Fox and was made executive producer. John Briley, the scriptwriter of *Gandhi*, had done a screenplay. Arthur didn't like it and did one himself, writing half of the 140-page script in two weeks. He also went to Los Angeles to consult about the cast and director, and had wanted Kenneth Branagh for the leading role. *The Crucible* was Arthur's great money-maker. Even before the film came out, the play had sold eight million paperback copies in America and was Penguin's best-selling book.

Arthur's older daughter, Jane (born in 1944), was married to a sculptor and lived in New York. In the early 1990s she and her husband built a house near Arthur's on land he gave them. He was proud of Rebecca, his daughter with Inge, born in 1962. Beautiful and talented, educated at Choate and Yale, she learned three languages and graduated *cum laude*. Two of her paintings appeared on the covers of the English editions of Arthur's *Collected Plays* and she had several exhibitions in New York. She had a successful career as an actress, writer, and director, justifying Arthur's belief that an actor did not need formal training of the Lee Strasberg kind. She appeared in a television series with Jack Lemmon; played (with one of Mailer's daughters) in Peter Brook's staging of Chekhov's *Three Sisters;* acted in *Consenting Adults* and other movies; designed the sets and directed the Cincinnati production of *After the Fall;* wrote and directed a mystical feature film, *Angela,* and two others scheduled for production. In 1996 Rebecca married Daniel Day-Lewis, son of the poet C. Day-Lewis and star of the movie version of *The Crucible.*

III

Arthur's life has a creative rhythm. He usually works for a few hours in the morning, then reads, does farm chores and carpentry, answers letters, and (in the summer) swims in his pond in the afternoon. He used to have a secretary, but he gave her up when he had to follow her schedule, not his. He switched to a computer for his autobiography, *Timebends,* and found it effective for revisions. He usually writes slowly and is preoccupied with the dramatic expression of his ideas.

Over the years Arthur often talked about his plays that were being revived. The idea for an early social protest play, *The Man Who Had All the Luck* (1944), came from Mary Slattery's rich and successful cousin in Ohio, who hanged himself at the age of twenty-eight. Arthur had alternate endings: in one the suicide was caused by fate, in the other by self-blame. *Focus* (1945), his novel about anti-Semitism, was published by an innovative firm, Reynal and Hitchcock, which folded when Hitchcock died young. Since Reynal supplied the money and they were not dependent on sales, they did as John Lehmann had done and as New Directions does today, publishing only books *they* liked to read.

Arthur's achievement came early in his life—though not quite so early as that of Fitzgerald or Hemingway—and many theater critics in the 1980s seemed to assume that his work was somehow "over," that there are no second acts for American writers. But the constant revivals show that his early plays still resonate, still matter. His first great success in the theater, *All My Sons* (1947), became popular in both Israel and Egypt after the war of 1967. Prime Minister Shimon Peres, who sat next to Arthur at the opening, told him it could have been a contemporary Israeli play. Some of his countrymen were also profiteering from arms sales while others risked their lives in the air. To the Israeli audience the play was not mere entertainment and, as a mark of respect for the solemnity of the occasion, they did not applaud at the end. In Sweden, too, the portrayal of war guilt in the play touched a nerve. The Swedes were still troubled by the fact that they had allowed Nazi troops to pass through their country to invade Norway in World War II.

Arthur said he wrote the famous scene in *The Misfits* (1961) in which Roslyn flirtatiously plays with a ball and paddle in a bar, but Marilyn did some improvising and gave it final form in the movie. He liked and admired John Huston, the director. He described him as tall, gangling, lively, macho, and adventurous, an expert with horses—an important skill in the movie—both sensitive and brutal. A good writer, with discriminating taste, he was less interested in the finer points of acting than in the composition of the scene.

Jane's Blanket (1963), an oddity and perhaps Miller's rarest book, is his only children's story, named after his older daughter. The poet-anthologist Louis Untermeyer asked him, as well as other well-known writers, to contribute to a series of children's books. Arthur knew only one story and wrote it in an hour. Each foreign edition had its own distinctive artwork.

Whenever I went to visit him, and in occasional letters, Arthur also kept me up-to-date about the progress of his current work. In September 1982 he was casting and preparing to direct two one-act plays, *I Can't Remember Anything* and *Clara,* at the Long Wharf theater in New Haven. The plays concerned "the limits of reality." One portrayed a man who enters a boutique to buy a gift for a dying friend; the other was about a detective and a prostitute who knows the truth about a man wrongly convicted of murder. By the time I first met him, Arthur had given up on serious theater on Broadway, which had become completely commercial. He had no plans to bring his new plays to New York, but involved himself instead with provincial theater and London productions.

The masterpiece of Arthur's late years is undoubtedly *Timebends* (1987). In a letter of April 1987, he said he was surprised and pleased with its reception: "I dreaded that its serpentine form . . . would put people off, but incredibly Book-of-the-Month has taken it," and it was translated into fifteen languages. Arthur had complained to me of the lack of historical background in the American reviews. My own review did not discuss the political side of Miller's life, but I noted the book's dominant themes: "the origins of creativity, the dangers of fame, the temptations of the flesh, the corruption of Hollywood, the commercialization of Broadway and the betrayal of American idealism." I explained that I was writing for William Buckley's conservative *National Review*—a magazine that would normally ignore the book—and that was not the place to discuss the communist witch-hunts of the 1950s.

The plot of the ironically titled film *Everybody Wins* (1990), originally called *Almost Everybody Wins*, was based on his one-act play *Some Kind of Love Story* (1984). In a New England mill town, a woman in her mid-thirties hires a private detective, an Irish ex-Chicago cop, to free a convicted murderer she knows to be innocent. The story explores the woman's multiple personalities which, for the detective, make all reality provisional. Though Arthur originally wanted Jack Nicholson for the leading role, the movie was made with Nick Nolte and Debra Winger. Though he's been in and out of the film business for years, Arthur remains psychologically detached from it. Movie stars who accumulate $50 million, he wryly observed, "become strange."

The Ride Down Mt. Morgan (1991) portrayed the confrontation of a wife and mistress around the hospital bed of a man who's had a car accident on an icy road. Arthur said it concerned the point at which an unpleasant but attractive man recognizes he's made a moral transgression. The play, like so many of his late works, is a mixture of the personal and subjective, the realistic and fantastic. He'd written more than a thousand pages of dialogue over a period of nine years before he knew where the play was going and could finish it—an interesting aside that tells us something of Miller's capacity to follow his urge, stick with an idea, and patiently develop it. The play was performed in London and Williamstown, and by the Public Theater in New York.

Arthur gladly signed all his books for me, and four of his inscriptions were illuminating. He wrote that *Situation Normal* (1944), his early book of military reportage, was "the first trigger pull." *In the Country* (1977), a charming book about Connecticut with photos by Inge, he called "This by now rare book and a favorite." He described the inspiration for *Everybody Wins* (1990) as "Things sometimes go whizzing off by themselves." And he linked the two settings of *The Archbishop's Ceiling* and *The American Clock*—an unnamed East European country (presumably Czechoslovakia) and the United States—by describing them as "two dangerously shaky, promising countries."

When I was writing the life of Scott Fitzgerald and describing his ill-fated career in Hollywood, I discussed the art of the screenplay with Arthur. He agreed with me that Joseph Mankiewicz was a much better screenwriter than Fitzgerald and had helped him by revising the script

of Erich Remarque's novel *Three Comrades*. In 1981 I had enthusiastically
suggested that Arthur write a screenplay of Joseph Conrad's *Victory*—
one of my favorite books. The system, he replied, did not encourage
even an established dramatist to write for the movies. A major studio
might pay him to do a script, but unless he owned the rights, the director could change it at will. In today's climate, it was highly unlikely
such a film would ever be made. Arthur could also raise the money
privately, but it would be risky. Investors expected to earn a 20 percent return; the cost of making a film like *Victory* would be too high,
its audience too small. And the star would always be more important
at the box office than Conrad or Miller. (Arthur was right about this,
as I discovered later on. Harold Pinter wrote a brilliant screenplay of
Victory, which was published but never produced. And Mark Peploe's
Victory (1995), with Willem Dafoe and Sam Neill, was held up by the
distributor, Miramax. They did not believe the film would make money
and never released it.)

                                    IV

Arthur didn't like teaching or lecturing, though he'd done a fair
amount of it. He found the Columbia students lively, those at Harvard and Yale surprisingly dull. He was pleased when a Columbia
student paid him a compliment by calling him truly "plugged in." At
the Harbourfront Writers' Conference in Toronto, he addressed 4,500
people in Symphony Hall—the first writer to speak there since 1938,
when Thomas Mann lectured after his arrival in North America. When
I tried to lure Arthur to the University of Colorado, he recalled that
he'd once attended their World Affairs conference and been given hospitality in a house where the marriage was clearly breaking up. He was
unwilling to return to Boulder because being lionized was boring, and
he dreaded the petty squabbles about the right to monopolize him.
    While on the subject of the academy, he remarked that none of the
biographical or critical books about him was any good and that several
of them were unreliable. Benjamin Nelson (1970) had mistakenly said
Arthur's mother had been a schoolteacher. James Goode (1963) had
missed the real story of *The Misfits*. His Japanese bibliographer, Tetsu-
maro Hayashi (1959), had hopelessly confused him with a cinematogra-
pher of the same name and made a hash of the attributions. Arthur was
especially critical of the Yale professor and *New Republic* drama critic
Robert Brustein. He had no sense of the theater but enormous power
to condemn a play, which was an expensive investment and had to at-

tract an increasingly cautious audience. Two critics Arthur approved
of were Harold Clurman, who'd coproduced *All My Sons* and directed
Incident at Vichy, and was for many years drama critic of the *Nation;*
and the younger English academic Christopher Bigsby, who ran the
Arthur Miller Theatre Studies Centre at the University of East Anglia
in Norwich.

Arthur always showed a friendly interest in my books, noted the
good reviews, and was generous with praise and letters of recommen-
dation. He even wrote a rare blurb for my life of Edmund Wilson,
which read in part: "I found it a fascinating exploration of a period and
the man who probably personified its critical intelligence and—most
of the time—its artistic conscience. Drunk or sober, in or out of love,
employed or not, Wilson was engaged with his time."

When he praised my book, I seized the opening to raise once again
the subject of his biography. He had a good excuse to turn me down—
his personal papers, in seven big filing cabinets that he daren't open,
were in a terrible mess. I countered, helpfully, that a good scholar or
librarian could do the organizing for him, and he admitted that Texas
had done an excellent job with his literary manuscripts. But this wasn't
the real reason for his reluctance. After two unhappy marriages and
a barrage of unfavorable publicity about Monroe, he couldn't face it.
Nor had he made any provision for a biography in his will, which
Inge would execute. He thought his remaining papers might go to the
Library of Congress or to the University of Michigan, where he got his
start as a playwright. Though he was at work on *Timebends* when we
had this conversation, he still maintained that his own life was dull.
The big problem, he said, was to make sense, form, and meaning of it
all. Leave it me, I said, that's what biographers do! He agreed that his
potential biography was important and that it ought to be done properly. I suggested he let me interview his family and friends (before it
was too late) and get started on a first volume that would take me up
to 1949. Superstitiously, he shook his head, exclaiming, "That's death!"

V

Just as the New York theater had changed for the worse in the course of
Arthur's career, so had the climate in publishing. He had had the same
agent for nearly forty years, and in that time ICM had been sold three
times. They had two rooms full of his records, so he couldn't leave them
even if he wanted to. But he did leave his publisher. Though Arthur's
books had sold in the millions, he complained of the way Viking was

treating him. The company had been bought by Penguin, an English firm owned by a German multinational corporation. Viking was run from London, with no one at the helm in New York. They had adopted a cost-accounting mentality and projected sales were estimated by marketing men who cared only for profits. His editor, Elizabeth Sifton, now lacked the power to push his work, and in this environment the author of quality books was no longer important. The day Arthur called Viking to discuss these issues, no one answered the phone for thirty rings. Neither the operator nor the secretary recognized his name.

He was furious that Viking didn't advertise *In the Country* (1977) after it received a negative review in the *New York Times Book Review*. At the same time that Graham Greene left Viking for Simon & Schuster and Saul Bellow left for Harper & Row, Arthur left them for Farrar, Straus & Giroux, which published *Chinese Encounters*, with photos by Inge, in 1979. But he was lured back to Viking with volumes of his *Theater Essays* and a second volume of his *Collected Plays*. He thought Viking's design of *"Salesman" in Beijing* (1984) was good, but the paper for the photographs was poor and so was the marketing. Voicing a complaint of all authors, he said the reviews were favorable, but the book was not available in the stores. He published with Aaron Asher at Grove Press between 1984 and 1990, when he again returned to Viking, which brought out his last three plays. *Homely Girl* (1995), his novella, had a first printing of only 6,000, but there was a surprising demand for the second printing of 25,000. It was being made into a film by a French company.

Arthur did not seem to read in a systematic fashion or deliberately seek material for plays, but took what came (or was sent) his way, what was recommended to him, or what interested him at the moment. He admired the work of J. F. Powers and Francis King, and copied down the title when I suggested Olivia Manning's *Balkan Trilogy*. He'd never been able to understand theosophy or how intelligent people could be gulled by "Buddhist bullshit." But he'd been absorbed in reading, for example, Torah stories with a commentary and excerpts from Schopenhauer in Rebecca's Yale textbook.

Over the years I often asked his opinion of other writers. For him, the positive and negative qualities of Wyndham Lewis's character canceled each other out, and he found it impossible to sympathize with him. Describing how Lewis, Hemingway, and many other modern writers felt obliged to kill the father figures in their fiction, he contrasted the European respect for the authoritarian father with the American desire to destroy the father and inability to assume his role.

He thought this was partly why most English and American writers lacked the "staying power" of a Thomas Mann. He recalled how he met Mann at a performance of *Death of a Salesman* in the late 1940s. Very formal in manner, Mann said in good but heavily accented English that he'd looked in vain for some philosophical statement in the play. Miller replied that he took pride in conveying his meaning through the action, without directly expressing a "message."

He acknowledged Hemingway as a stylistic, if not personal, in-fluence when he first started writing. In his view, Hemingway trans-formed the American idiom into a literary language, and virtually every American writer, except for the Southerners who followed Faulkner, was influenced by him. Arthur didn't know that Edmund Wilson had written eight plays and been married to the actress Mary Blair, who'd appeared in many O'Neill plays, but called Wilson "the best critic we ever had." He described Wilson's late mistress, the screenwriter and film critic Penelope Gilliatt (who'd been married to John Osborne), as not especially attractive and a very heavy drinker. He thought Wilson's surprising connection with Lillian Hellman was based on mutual love of gossip. He blasted Hellman for her intellectual dishonesty—and felt she fully deserved the attacks by Mary McCarthy, Martha Gellhorn, and Diana Trilling. Hellman was also an imperious hostess on Martha's Vineyard. When Styron invented an excuse to avoid her dinner party and she discovered the truth (at the store where they both shopped for fancy desserts), she didn't speak to him for a year.

When he talked about writers he seemed especially concerned with personal character, and made shrewd judgments about the contrast be-tween art and message, between the quality of an author's work and his literary reputation. Wise and benign himself, Arthur was fascinated by good writers, like V. S. Naipaul, who were famous for being nasty. John Osborne and Philip Roth, desperate to antagonize their audience, were deliberately offensive in their work and behavior. (He was sure none of these nasties received as many begging letters as he did.) But he liked Roth (a summer neighbor) personally, was amused by his nasty side, and didn't presume to judge him.

Describing a dinner with Alexander Solzhenitsyn at the Connecti-cut house of his translator Thomas Whitney, Arthur said the Russian spoke no English and only a little German, and the host translated for him. Imperious, authoritative, and dictatorial, he was unappealing but impressive. His didactic manner, inherited from Tolstoy, made him more concerned with message than with art, but his honest vehemence and personal courage gave him real power. Arthur praised his noble vision, but felt living under his government wouldn't be pleasant. He thought East European writers like Solzhenitsyn and Kosinski, more ideologues than artists, craved power themselves even as they criticized the powers that be.

I was interested in Arthur's appraisals of the contemporary theater and asked him to reflect on the playwrights of his youth. He said the popular, melodramatic, and now neglected playwright David Belasco actually taught the influential Russian director Konstantin Stanislavsky a good deal about theatrical realism. In the 1930s Eugene O'Neill, who had been so great in the previous decade and had lived until 1953, seemed completely dated and had dropped into oblivion. *A Moon for the Misbegotten* (1957), like many of his plays, had flat language and a stale plot. His greatest work was the posthumously published *Long Day's Journey Into Night* (1956).

Clifford Odets had suffered the same fate as O'Neill. Though Odets had invented contemporary realistic New York speech and was often imitated, he didn't transcend his time and was now dull and dated. Odets knew Miller slightly, but resented him for eclipsing his star. Arthur disliked the long biography of Odets (1982) by the psychoanalyst Margaret Brenman-Gibson and felt it was too long, doting, and subjective a book.

By contrast, he admired the underrated Tennessee Williams—with whom he had a passing acquaintance and who seemed to have mainly homosexual friends—and believed his works would last. Unlike Williams, Edward Albee had been relatively silent at the time of our interview. Both had had to find their way into a heterosexual world from the suppressed homosexual one.

Harold Pinter, a close friend, was by temperament always angry and embittered. But in 1993 he had a new play, *Moonlight,* coming out in London, which Arthur had read in typescript and thought was very good. *Glengarry Glen Ross* (1983) by David Mamet, one of the stars of contemporary American stage and film, had powerful language and theatrical effects, including crude and shocking language. But, unlike Arthur, brought up in the idealistic 1930s, the much younger Mamet had by main force to create some kind of "moral vessel" into which he could distill his ideas.

Saul Bellow was an old friend. In 1956, when they were both waiting in Reno for a divorce, they lived in neighboring cabins. Their common editor at Viking, Pascal Covici, suggested they go west together and keep each other company. (At that time the place seemed remote, and they were surrounded by Indians. A few years later, when he returned to film *The Misfits,* everything had changed and Reno was booming.) He was impressed by Bellow's erudition, which Bellow casually tried to hide. Though part of the academic establishment at the University of Chicago, Bellow disliked the scholarly and academic world. In May 1986, after learning about yet another divorce, Arthur wrote, "I was sorry to hear about Bellow, had thought from reports that was a reasonable marriage, but I guess he will have to go on to the end writing new chapters."

Like most writers, Arthur was fascinated by the manic character of Robert Lowell, whom he'd met in the political turmoil of the 1960s. A wildly disconnected speaker, a terrible snob, sometimes crazy and cruel, Lowell also had a winning and sympathetic personality. When I sent my book *Manic Power: Robert Lowell and His Circle* (1987)—which was dedicated to him—Arthur saw (as few others did) the significance of the interwoven chapters that I had used to structure the work: "I found that by reflecting Lowell's illness in and among that group of writers a kind of epochal sense emerged, and in a way that was otherwise impossible one got the feeling that his illness was something more than personal."

I was curious to ask Miller, a veteran insider, panel member, and literary judge, about how prizes to writers were awarded. This topic made him smile with a gentle cynicism. Some prizes, he said, were finally given because the committee had failed to reach an agreement by five o'clock and, desperate for a pee and a drink, simply gave in to whoever persisted with his pet candidate. We got on to Mailer's Pulitzer Prize for *The Executioner's Song* (1980) and the prize awarded to a journalist who had falsified her stories. Basically, he said, prizes were useless. No one today would recognize 98 percent of the plays that had won the Pulitzer. He'd won it for *Death of a Salesman,* but not for *The Crucible,* which was considered too left-wing.

For years I had wondered why certain obviously great writers, Miller especially, did not win the biggest one of all, the Nobel Prize. Arthur agreed that many undeserving authors had won it and thought that Graham Greene was the most overlooked contender. (He felt Greene's artistic failure in *Monsignor Quixote* [1982] was caused more by his preachy Catholic doctrine than by lack of literary inspiration.) Arthur told me how, during the run of one of his plays at the National Theatre in London, the publicity office heard a rumor that he'd won the Nobel Prize. As they started to exploit the story, the rumor proved false. He had never expected to receive the prize, despite his worldwide success and the enduring appeal of his classic plays, but he'd heard that some writers (Octavio Paz, for example, who won it in 1990) had actively electioneered for it. He predicted a Chinese writer would get it soon. I added that coming from a major country that had never won the prize was a great advantage, and considered Margaret Atwood of Canada and Jorge Amado of Brazil strong candidates. Because political persecution was another important (and nonliterary) criterion, I thought Salman Rushdie, Ariel Dorfman, and Vaclav Havel were also in the running. Arthur was amused by this Nobel racecard, but clearly wasted no sleep over it.

VI

Always in demand, in the 1980s and 1990s Arthur became a sort of independent cultural ambassador, a representative of the respectable American Left, a survivor of a time when writers were forced to take sides. As one who has endured morally and artistically, he receives lots of high-profile invitations and has opportunities accorded few writers. In 1981, he flew to Paris on a Concorde, a guest of the French government, to attend President François Mitterand's inauguration, to which only scientists, artists, and writers—among them Styron, Gabriel García Márquez, and Julio Cortázar—were invited. People were dressed informally at the impressive ceremony, and he had the opportunity to talk to Mitterand. In 1993 he and Inge were invited to Buenos Aires and Bariloche, where a Jewish-Argentine bank had asked him to lecture on civil rights and artistic expression. President Carlos Menem had finally stabilized the currency and (contra Naipaul's pessimistic reports in the *New York Review of Books* of January 1992) the country seemed fairly prosperous.

Arthur and Inge were particularly enthusiastic about China. In 1982 he was planning to return to direct a production of *Death of a Salesman* with the aid of an expert interpreter and friend, Cao Yu, who'd been studying in Missouri. (This experience he described in *"Salesman" in Beijing.*) In communist countries Miller's plays assumed the vivid political dimensions they had in their first American productions. The Chinese especially took theater very seriously and looked for the political message in everything. In Shanghai (home of the Gang of Six) *The Crucible* made no impression, but in Beijing they interpreted the play in terms of the Cultural Revolution and were deeply moved. Arthur said he disliked the Russians' anti-Semitism and general unpleasantness, and would not return to their country. He found the Chinese more open and honest, despite a standard of living so low that by Western standards most people were starving.

Miller's experience of the ideological battles of the past made his presence valuable in PEN, the international writers' organization. In 1981 he attended a conference at which the conservative writer Midge Decter, claiming that communist-inspired journalists were deliberately writing lies, advocated the creation of a new Un-American Activities Committee. Appalled, Arthur felt the New York intellectual scene, once his home ground, was fast becoming unintelligible to him. He told the audience the story of a seventeenth-century Puritan who maintained that a woman accused of witchcraft had in fact been good and kind to everyone. Cotton Mather replied, "God thought the Devil was beautiful and good one hour before he fell." These quotes brought the house down, and when he asked, "Do we have to go through all this *again* —not just Joe McCarthy, but Cotton Mather?" Decter backed down. As East Europe became intellectually freer, America seemed to become more conformist. In an interview with Nelson Mandela in South Africa, Arthur noted that South African universities couldn't get away with the oppressive political correctness and ideological indoctrination going on in America.

In 1985 Arthur was elected president of PEN International, and after completing his term he confined his political activities to signing a few important petitions and trying to help East European writers get out of jail. In those days communist governments feared economic reprisals from the West and responded to protests from influential writers. In 1985, sponsored by PEN, he and Harold Pinter traveled to Turkey to help writers jailed for "political offenses." Pinter had a fiercely effective temper and exploded at a dinner with the American ambassador. The government wouldn't see them, but they met the opposition, tried to exert some humane pressure, and later heard that prison conditions had slightly improved. His article describing this journey was first accepted, then rejected, by the conservative *New York Times*, and was finally published in the *Nation* and the London *Observer*.

The McCarthy period had cost Arthur a close friend and colleague, Elia Kazan. Unlike Miller, he'd named names before the HUAC, and the two had quarreled bitterly. Kazan's *A Life* (1988) was full of gaps, lies, and self-justifications. He said that Miller had "walked away from" their film *The Hook*. In fact, Miller had refused to turn the gangsters into communists, as the Columbia Pictures mogul Harry Cohn and the Hollywood union bosses wanted him to do. The film was later rewritten that way by Budd Schulberg (another self-serving "friendly witness") as *On the Waterfront*. Kazan, still racked by guilt about his be-trayal of close friends, once stared at a fellow writer and asked, "You're thinking about it, aren't you?" He ascribed his behavior to some mys-tical racial memory. As a Greek in Turkey, Kazan said, he had to learn the art of survival. Morality, honor, and personal courage—or so his story went—were much less important than looking after oneself.

Far from doctrinaire, however, Arthur saw the moral and human complexities of these times. In 1996 I was writing a life of Humphrey Bogart, who in 1947 first opposed and then recanted his opposition to HUAC, and sought Arthur's opinion of his behavior. (Arthur himself appeared before the Committee in 1956, when anti-communist hysteria was at its height.) He thought Bogart had been misled by the Holly-wood Ten, who'd been called before the Committee but did not tell him that they were in fact communists. Bogart rightly feared the witch-hunt would end his career, and Miller was "reluctant to judge him in this two-edged story."

VII

Perhaps the most sensitive issue I discussed with Arthur, and to me the saddest, was the question of his literary reputation at home. Ameri-can theater critics had savagely expressed the belief that since *After the Fall* in 1964, Miller's plays—like those of O'Neill, Odets, and Osborne—had abruptly declined. For many years Arthur has been in the unique position of being more appreciated, and certainly more performed, in England than in America. In June 1984, on a triumphant visit, he read from *"Salesman" in Beijing* to overflow audiences at the National The-atre and the University of East Anglia, where he received an honor-ary degree. He dined with the novelist Angus Wilson, and had a pene-trating radio interview on the BBC's "Kaleidoscope." He contrasted the well-prepared English journalists with the Americans, who barely glanced at the book before the program went on the air and didn't have a clue what questions to ask. The most intelligent reviews of his work appeared in the London *Spectator*. On his eightieth birthday, in 1995, Oxford University awarded him another honorary degree.

We often discussed the difference between the American and Eng-lish theater. He thought English directors, like Bill Bryden, tried to bring out the best in a play, while the more egoistic Americans wanted to put their personal stamp on it. He contrasted the elevated style of English acting to the limited realism of the Americans. Expressive actors, like Dustin Hoffman, Robert De Niro, Al Pacino, and Harvey Keitel, were very good at confrontational parts, but British players, trained on Shakespeare, had much greater range and skill. He particularly admired Anthony Hopkins in the National Theatre production of *Pravda* and in the film *The Silence of the Lambs*.

Arthur emphasized the comparatively low cost of putting on plays in England. Cameron MacIntosh, producer of the phenomenally successful Andrew Lloyd Webber musicals, told him that New York theaters cost three times as much as the ones in London. The London production of O'Neill's *Mourning Becomes Electra*, with Glenda Jackson, cost $100,000. When the play came to New York, the backers had to pay $600,000 before the curtain went up. Noting that Lincoln Center was currently dark, he concluded that there was simply much greater opportunity for serious theater in England.

Arthur is not uncritical of England. He satirized the upper-class twits he'd observed at a sherry party in London and, at the opposite end of the scale, the six flat-capped workers, supposedly connecting a water pipe to a fountain at John Huston's castle in Ireland. For three years they dug and shifted dirt around, under the tolerant eye of the master. He remembered how English unions, with their interminable delays and tea breaks, had almost ruined the Monroe–Olivier film *The Prince and the Showgirl* (1957). "The more I learn about England," he wrote me in September 1990, "the harder it is to understand why [anyone] lives there . . . even though I find myself loving it in a perverse way." Keen to "reach people who wouldn't normally go to the theater," he praised the responsive audiences in London. Reflecting on his own experience, he once observed that "the American theater was more valued abroad than at home."

In the late 1940s, he recalled, he'd visited his college roommate in Little Rock, Arkansas, and heard great backwoods storytellers, who attracted large crowds. NBC found out about them, but they refused to come to New York. The problem today is that such regional artists no longer exist, and even if they did, nobody would be interested. Literary and theatrical life has become purely commercial. Citing the recent New York closing of Pinter's play, *The Hothouse*, which got rave reviews, Arthur said it was now impossible to make money on intellectually challenging drama. Theater tickets in New York now cost as much as a night at the Stork Club and customers expect the same kind of fun for their money. The serious audience has almost disappeared. During the last decade, however, the tide has turned strongly in his favor. The Tony Award for the revival of *A View from the Bridge,* its transfer to Broadway from a limited run at the Roundabout, and its national tour have led to a new appreciation of his artistic achievement.

Though Arthur has not lost his idealistic belief in the social importance of the theater, he is pessimistic about the future of books and plays in a world that regards every literary work as an investment, meant to generate cash. He laments the alienation of artists from society and from each other in the cutthroat, fearful atmosphere of today. In his view, the discontinuity in American intellectual life reflects the wider lack of a collective memory and a collective culture.

4

Iris Murdoch

1919 born in Dublin
1942 graduates from Somerville College, Oxford
1954 *Under the Net*
1956 marries John Bayley
1961 *A Severed Head*
1978 *The Sea, The Sea*
1999 dies in London

I

I had always admired the qualities that made Iris Murdoch a great novelist: her technical skill, richness of imagination, philosophical ideas, moral vision. Reviewing *A Fairly Honourable Defeat* in the *Boston Globe* in February 1970, I praised the "compassionate intelligence that asserts the possibilities, however frail, of human love." When I sent her the review, she wrote encouragingly that my interpretation of the novel was "on the right lines." She suggested we meet when I next came to England, but I did not feel I knew her well enough to follow up the invitation.

In March 1978 I had a second chance. Iris and her husband, John Bayley, Warton Professor of English at Oxford, were invited to teach at the University of Denver. They each gave a public lecture—Iris on "Art Imitates Nature," John on "Hardy's Poetry"—and jointly led a two-week seminar on "Truth and Falsehood in Fiction." When my wife and I drove in to attend the seminar from nearby Boulder, where we were both teaching, we were surprised to find only three other participants. We wondered if the locals were too intimidated to attend a class taught by what journalists had called "the most intelligent couple in the world."

The dimly lit seminar room gave me my first glimpse of them. John, like Professor Calculus in the Tin-Tin books, was short and bald, with little wings of hair on the sides of his head. He had untied shoelaces and mismatched socks, a stained woolly tie and fly at half-mast. Soft-voiced and benign, he managed to steer his dazzling talk through an alarming, even spectacular stutter. Photographs of Iris in her twenties reveal that she'd been a great beauty, and in her youth many Oxford men had fallen in love with her. Though bulky now, at sixty, she was still attractive. She had a charming expression, serene yet alert and curious, with short, roughly cut hair; bright, clear-seeing eyes; and (as I later discovered when I kissed her cheek) soft, rosy skin. Her dress was donnish and distinctly nonfashionable: full skirts and shapeless smocks, dark stockings and sensible shoes. Like the title of one of her novels, she seemed both nice and good.

Their seminar focused on the form of the novel, especially in Tolstoy, Dostoyevsky, and Mauriac's *Thérèse Desqueyroux*, which luckily I had just read. But their talk ranged freely over all sorts of novels, and they responded easily to any topic the students raised. The intimate class allowed me to observe their brilliant, provocative, even mesmerizing teaching, both when engaged with each other in an intellectual duet and when they questioned and stimulated us to keep up with them. As in the best kind of tutorial, they raised the students to the level of the teacher by sharing their ideas and creating a collaborative atmosphere. Humane and highly civilized, both combined penetrating—yet entertaining—knowledge of the form, characters, and ideas of the novels with down-to-earth and humanly engaging analysis of the meaning. Ever-present in the discussion was the deeper structure of the novels, the presence of the author's mind and spirit. In contrast to the linguistic critics, who have largely replaced this type of moral teaching, they recreated and enhanced the experience of reading and invited the students to share their responses.

The Rocky Mountain spring was capricious as ever, and slush and ice had lined the streets. As guests of the university, Iris and John had been cloistered in Denver. They were eager to break out of the Brown Palace Hotel and see a bit more of Colorado, and agreed to come and spend some time with us in Boulder. On April 4, an exceptionally warm and bright spring day, I took them on a campus tour. In our wool jackets and scarves, we gazed down at the students, bronzed already, sunning themselves in bathing suits in the pool patio. I pointed out some of the stranger sights of the university: the office of the Gay–Lesbian Caucus (then a rarity for a college campus), the robotic lap-swimmers in the Olympic-sized pool, the grunting brutes in the weightlifting room, the surrealistic ice rink, and the Alferd Packer Grill —ghoulishly named for a convicted cannibal, who was snowed in one winter and forced to survive by eating his companions. At lunch I introduced Iris to the bagel.

Warm-hearted and sympathetic, Iris was ready to discuss any subject, and had the novelist's curiosity about new people and places. At a small party we held, she talked to everyone, tried to draw each person out, and listened attentively to what they had to say. That day our conversation ranged over a number of topics, and we discussed both her novels and her life. Among contemporary writers she admired Saul Bellow and Philip Larkin. When I asked her why she had so many homosexual characters in her novels, she said she knew so many of them at Oxford. She did not use foreign settings because she had not lived abroad long enough to feel she'd thoroughly understood an alien locale. Her only extended residence in a foreign country was when she had worked with refugees in Austria after the war. I had noted that she was keenly interested in paintings and liked to bring them into her fiction, and we talked about the German expressionist Max Beckmann, whom she'd used in *Henry and Cato*. In the novel, the hero plans to write a book about the painter. Her interest in Beckmann continued, and in July 1985 she wrote: "What a great painter—I love him—we saw a lot of his work in [the] St. Louis Art Museum, and saw a good deal of private stuff too, property of one Buster May. (He is dead now alas—I hope he left the paintings to the Art Museum.) Just lately we came across 6 wonderful Beckmanns in the Museum in Cologne."

I asked about her attitude to reviews, and she said they weren't sent to her and she rarely read them. She felt that they were usually hasty and superficial, that often reviewers and critics did not understand what her books were really about. She liked her longtime publisher, Chatto & Windus, and spoke well of the editor D. J. Enright. She had no literary agent for her novels; felt her dramatic agent was poor and wanted to get another one. She had received a modest advance of $2,000 from Viking for her latest novel, *Henry and Cato* (1976), and earned only $600 in American royalties in 1977.

We also talked about Boulder and college life in general. She disapproved of the current sexual morality of students and felt it would be better if there were less promiscuity. Abortion centers made men more careless and placed more responsibility for pregnancy on women. When I mentioned that Boulder was the center of American Buddhism and that a Tibetan lama taught there, she knew that "Rinpoche" meant "precious one." She was "nearly a Buddhist" herself, would follow the lama if she lived near him, and concluded that Buddhism was "the best of all religions."

II

After that first meeting Iris wrote me, over the next eighteen years, 110 letters. We met nine more times in London and Oxford, and I interviewed her for the *Paris Review* "Writers at Work" series. In that time she published a dozen books of philosophy, fiction, poetry, and drama; lectured around the world; won the Booker Prize; and became Dame Iris. She was a faithful correspondent whose letters, sprinkled with exclamation marks and written in an extraordinarily difficult hand, I slowly deciphered. (She decorated one particularly jolly letter with a wavy aquamarine border and five red stars.) But she had to be stimulated with questions that interested and provoked her—especially printed comments about her behavior and private life—or she would simply, when pressed for time, dash off a quick note. (I never got her to explain, for example, why many philosophers thought Herbert Spencer was important.) There was, I think, a maternal–filial element in our friendship, and she always signed off with "love," "much love," or "lots of love."

When we first met my daughter was only six. Over the years Iris took a lively interest in her academic progress and achievements, and hoped she'd come to Oxford after graduating from Swarthmore. My daughter loved the beach, and Iris often mentioned, in her late letters, the pleasures of swimming—as child and adult—in the ocean, rivers, and lakes. While on holiday in Dorset during a heat wave, she'd spent most of her time in the sea. She thought Oxford would be perfect if it could be "removed" and placed near the sea, and dreamed of having her own swimming pool.

She was twenty years older than me and a world-famous writer, yet we had some literary and academic friends in common. I was keenly interested in her work and in the literary scene in general, and eagerly absorbed all she had to say. I was also an energetic and productive writer, though of a different sort. She discussed the authors I was writing about, encouraged me, and praised my books, and I always wanted to please her. She liked the fact that I worked hard and got the job done. Unlike some critics, she never thought I wrote too fast and too much. "Now to [Scott] Fitzgerald," she wrote in March 1993, "410 pages in 4 months—I cd never manage that. You are a great power house."

Though they must have had many books dedicated to them, Iris and John seemed pleased when they wrote to accept the dedication of one of my biographies. "<u>Yes</u>, we wd be very glad indeed and proud to be dedicatees of your Hemingway! We shall be delighted to see ourselves in real print inside your book. . . . Thanks again so much for your thought about the book. It's a most cheering and lovely event!" When I sent them a copy, she replied: "It is so kind of you—and we feel so proud! It's a very special and moving present, and we are delighted!"

It was always her way to praise and encourage. I once rather cheekily sent her a story I had written (and later published) about the last days of Gerald Brenan—an authority on Spain whom I knew and admired. She called it "moving and elegant and sad and full of atmosphere. You must write a lot more stories." Treasuring this remark, I mailed the story to another friend, the novelist J. F. Powers, who sent me an exasperated (and no doubt more accurate) appraisal.

One of my essays, "The Nobel Prize and Literary Politics" (*DLB Yearbook: 1988*), elicited a lively response from her: "I read your Nobel prize piece with great interest and pleasure, and was amazed and thrilled and delighted when I reached the last sentence! [Murdoch is "the most worthy and promising candidate for the Nobel Prize."] How kind of you to think of me here and utter those friendly generous thoughts. I am quite overcome. . . . I boast that I met a rarely seen winner of that prize, Halldór Laxness, in his remote snowbound house in Iceland. We had a merry drunken time." Though Iris liked a drink before dinner and a bottle of wine with her meal, I never had the pleasure of seeing her merrily drunk.

At one time I suggested editing a Viking *Portable Murdoch*, sent her a table of contents, and asked for her comments. Evidently against the idea, she did not reply, and our correspondence lapsed. (Her essays were finally collected in a weighty tome, *Existentialists and Mystics*, 1997.) Three months later, wrongly thinking that I was "cross" with her, she wrote an especially long and interesting letter to placate me.

One project she did allow was my *Paris Review* interview, which I recorded in July 1988 at her house on Hamilton Road in Oxford. The first floor sitting room, which led out to the garden, had a gas fire and a well-stocked bar. There were paintings and tapestries of flowers, art books and records, pottery and glassware, embroidered cushions on the deep sofa. We did the interview in her paper-strewn second-floor study, decorated with oriental rugs and with paintings of horses and children, overlooking the apple and birch trees in the carefully tended garden.

Her manner, as always, was gentle but firm. Experienced at interviews, Iris gave, without coaxing, thoughtful, elaborate answers. She spoke extensively about her life and about larger questions: art, philosophy, morality, and religion. But she told me next to nothing about her work habits and creative process, and was guarded about the sources and meaning of specific novels. (This would prove to be a bone of contention with the magazine.) As a friend, I was reluctant to press her—I didn't ask, for example, why she had never had children—as I would have done if I'd known her less well. Afterwards we went out to lunch at her local Italian restaurant.

Once the interview was transcribed, Iris revised and expanded it, deleting and adding whole paragraphs, and including an entire new page of manuscript. But she could not do it right away, and did not elaborate on the particular points I raised. On October 1 she wrote: "I have looked at it and I think it will take a long time to check it—all minor things, possibly not rewarding, and may need thought. . . . Sorry not to respond at once—will deal with the interview before too long I hope." She sent the revisions on October 24.

In December I was distressed to hear that the *Paris Review* would publish the interview only if Iris were willing to answer even more questions, in writing and in her own good time. If she were not willing, they probably would not. When I told her about this she wrote back with uncharacteristic anger: "I am amazed. Who do these Paris Review people think they are? Are they French or Americans? Why do they think they're so grand. I thought they'd commissioned the thing. I'm not at all sure I want to answer their questions. It depends on what the questions are. You may say that I will consider their questions. (Yes, I realise we have spent some time on this operation and it would be a pity to lose it!)" Iris certainly knew who she was, what she had achieved, and how she stood in the literary world. She also had strict ideas about proper behavior and a streak of genuine humility. Reflecting on her previous outburst in the following month, she added: "About the Paris Review—I was only being jokily ironical in my last letter. The bit of substance was that I was willing to look at their extra questions! I hope they have not got the impression of me as a sort of touchy grandee, which I am certainly not!"

I finally persuaded the *Paris Review* to publish the interview without further response from Iris, and wrote to tell her so. Meanwhile, however, as she explained in a charmingly contrite letter of February 25, 1989, she had unwittingly complicated and confused my delicate negotiations:

I'm afraid I did write a very nice note to Paris Review (some time before receiving your letter of Feb 19) to say I was glad to hear they were going to publish the piece, and that if they still wanted to ask questions I wd consider them. As they had definitely decided to publish, I thought an olive branch, or oil on waters, move was in place. I'm sorry, and now wish I hadn't, and do hope that won't delay things further—I feel pretty sure it won't, I haven't heard from them, and my note was vague and merely friendly! I'm sorry too I didn't answer your additional queries—I can't recall this exactly—I hope you are not cross with me, please say you are not. . . . Once more, I'm sorry about the P Review matter and apologise for rushing in!

I was surprised that Iris felt the need to apologize and touched by her concern for my feelings.

As it happened, Iris *did* answer some additional questions, after a lecture she gave in New York, and the editors inserted this extra material into the interview. This caused more friction. The questioner wanted his name to appear with mine as the author of the piece, and I had to fight to delete it. Eventually the magazine cut our interview in half, without consulting me, and did not publish it until the summer of 1990.

III

In one respect, our correspondence continued the Denver seminar indefinitely, ranging from classic authors—Lady Murasaki to John Cowper Powys (a great favorite and, I suspect, a strong influence on her work)—to prominent academics and friends like Lord Glenavy, the philosopher A. J. Ayer, and the United Nations official Brian Urquhart. I often asked her what she thought of contemporary writers. Iris recalled that in 1954 she and John had met Edmund Wilson "in Oxford I think chez Isaiah Berlin, in a dark room. He was rather tough & forbidding and he frightened me. I think Mary McCarthy was with him, or perhaps I dreamed that"—which she certainly did, as Wilson and McCarthy were divorced in 1946. I had always wondered why Wilson had pronounced both Iris and John "boring." They were evidently too intimidated by his fierce reputation and forbidding demeanor to contribute much to the conversation.

I especially wanted to know what Iris thought of T. E. Lawrence, D. H. Lawrence, and Joseph Conrad, writers important to me. Alluding perhaps to T. E.'s association with British imperialism in the Middle East or to his habit of backing into the limelight, she wrote in 1990, two years after his centenary: "I love T. E. Lawrence, who seems to be hated by many people here [in England]. (I also detest D. H. Lawrence, the chap not the books, who seems to be worshipped by many people here!)" I also asked if she knew of a woman doctor in Oxford who had been D. H. Lawrence's pupil as a child. "How awful to be tutored by D. H. Lawrence!" she exclaimed, disapproving of his didactic, mystical, and misogynistic streak. In my next letter I countered this by arguing that D. H. was a brilliantly innovative and successful teacher, both in schools and private tutorials. Responsive to argument and willing to be challenged, Iris replied with engaging humility: "Yes, I daresay Lawrence was an inspiring teacher. I spoke out of prejudice! (I don't altogether like the personality of the author. . . . A genius of course & a lovely writer.)"

In another illuminating passage she contrasted Lawrence with Conrad: "DHL is a great writer but I don't (I confess) altogether like him. I like Kangaroo best, and some of the stories and poems. But I cannot love him and don't like his attitudes. I find Conrad a more congenial and possibly greater writer. I think Lord Jim is [a] wonderful novel. I read it again lately and was very deeply moved by it—including the latter part which some say is less good." In conversation, she rejected John's idea that Lord Jim was really a Pole and therefore rather unconvincing as an adventurous Englishman.

I once asked how Plato's belief (quoted by Iris in *The Fire and the Sun*) that a good book must be produced by a good character related to modern writers, who often had bad characters yet wrote good books. Didn't Malcolm Lowry use his own bad character to give considerable power to *Under the Volcano*? She agreed, but argued that Lawrence's faults of character led to faults in his books. She did not agree that Kafka had a bad (that is, a weak) character, but said—despite his self-condemnations—that his strong, noble character accounted for the greatness of his books.

Occasionally Iris sent me interesting tidbits from her Oxford life. The avant-garde Bulgarian critic Tzvetan Todorov, "an awfully nice chap, came to give the Bateman lecture, and produced a good old fashioned academic speech, to the disappointment of the young Turks." She criticized narcissistic academic conferences, where "one must become a detached spectator, meditating upon human folly," but said she sometimes met sympathetic souls when attending them. At a forthcoming PEN conference in Cambridge she hoped to meet again "that enchanting boy Vikram Seth (author of the great Californian novel, in verse [*The Golden Gate*], in the metre of Eugene Onegin). I met him in Delhi last year [1987] and liked him very much, a very talented & charming fellow."

In June 1987 she sent a portrait of A. N. Wilson, who had, on and off, been writing her biography:

> I'm glad you like Andrew Wilson's novels. He is a former pupil of John's, wanted to be an Anglican priest, but then decided not, used to teach in Oxford, but now is freelance literary man (perhaps still does a little teaching). He's married to a clever girl who is an English don, fellow of Somerville (Katherine Duncan-Jones). They are both very nice. His latest novel (called <u>Stray</u>) is written from the point of view of a cat. I've read three of his novels, with great pleasure—I think he's very good & getting better.

IV

Like many successful and respected writers, Iris was sometimes torn by the need for privacy and quiet in which to write, and the natural desire to see people and travel the world. In the years I knew her she was frequently invited to attend conferences and lecture abroad. Though these meetings interfered with her work, she accepted most offers, enjoying her role as famous novelist and, at the same time, observing "human folly." Pondering her frenetic activity, she asked: "Why does one do it (go away)? Staying home and working quietly is much jollier." But staying home meant subjecting herself and her work to scrutiny. There were scores of books and articles about her, many, she felt, written by well-intentioned people. But she thought most criticism of her work was absurd. She especially mocked a computer study that had counted the number of times the word "virgin" appeared in her novels. Ignoring it as much as possible, she confessed, "I can't read books about myself."

Inevitably she also became victimized by the type of article that pays homage to the great writer and pretends to intimate knowledge of the subject, while including as much disparaging gossip or scandalous trivia as it can find. Annoyed by a condescending and satiric piece by James Atlas, published in March 1988, I offered to send it to her. Atlas had quoted the Oxford don Sir Maurice Bowra, a well-known homosexual, who had—maliciously and quite absurdly—said of Iris and John: "Lovely couple. I've slept with both of them." She replied with some irritation and a little sorrow, though her habit of ignoring critics was unshaken: "I have not seen the Vanity Fair article (and don't want to). Too bad we sound so drunk & decrepit. What a fascinating remark by Bowra!" Iris dismissed what she ironically called his "charming witticism" and insisted it was "untrue of course."

Iris was irritated once again when the tabloid *Daily Mail* published a sensational but revealing "interview" with her on June 5, 1988. It described her love affair with the handsome war hero Frank Thompson, an Oxford graduate who was captured and executed behind enemy lines in Nazi-occupied Bulgaria. It appeared with a photograph of Iris and the Czech refugee-anthropologist Franz Steiner, who—with Eduard Fraenkel, Arnoldo Momigliano, and Elias Canetti—was one of her older European gurus. "I gave no interview to the Daily Mail," she wrote. "The first I heard of their article was when somebody said they'd seen it, and I got hold of a copy. The Mail never communicated with me or sent me a copy of the piece. Such are the ways of journalists. . . . About Frank, there is a lot of general knowledge. I can't imagine where the picture of Franz with me came from!"

She was also disturbed by a nasty little notice in the *Sunday Times* in March 1991, which falsely suggested that she had quarreled with A. N. Wilson and betrayed his friendship by selling a book he had inscribed to her and John. Iris then explained what really happened: "I'm sorry about what the ST said—We certainly did not intend to sell our presentation copies of A. W. We keep all such. We received several copies of the book on publication, and must have for once set aside the wrong one for sale. I regret that very much. There is no end to the spite of journalists."

As an eminent cultural figure Iris was the subject of official portraits, and had decided views on how she should be presented. St. Anne's, where she had taught philosophy, had commissioned her portrait by an Austrian, Marie-Louise Moteseczky, but didn't like the finished product. But Iris did, so she bought it from the artist for £500 and presented it to the college. Another rather beautiful painting of her, by Tom Phillips, in the National Portrait Gallery, she liked enough to reproduce on the dust wrapper of *The Green Knight* and later novels. But she hated the photograph that Arnold Newman took for the *Sunday Times'* "Great British" exhibition in December 1979. Guarding her privacy, she didn't want photographers and journalists "to look at my things," and sat for him at her publishers'. Newman seemed put out that she'd refused to invite him to her home. Though there were many pleasant book-filled rooms at Chatto & Windus, he insisted on using an empty corridor that was being painted. She thought him superficial and phony, relying on props and with no real interest in the faces of his subjects. In the finished photo she stands in front of a bare white wall, clasps her arms to her breast, and stares angrily at the camera.

John and Iris always seemed to me a particularly devoted and harmonious couple, so I was alarmed when a London friend relayed rumors that their marriage was breaking up. I wrote to her about it and she replied: "I am amazed that someone has suggested that John and I are parted, divorced, this is absolutely impossible, we are utterly loving and forever together and well known to be, and have always been! Not an 'oddity'—a perfect marriage—if that's odd! Please tell the crazy someone that it is a completely happy marriage, and he or she need not worry! I would be sorry if this false news 'went around.'" I did my best to suppress this malicious rumor. As she justly wrote in another context, "We must not take for granted that good and rational and generous behaviour, concern for others, can be relied upon and will spread throughout the world."

On another occasion we discussed a more damaging and insidious misconception. I asked Iris about a passage in Victoria Glendinning's life of Rebecca West that stated, "West believed that Iris Murdoch's *The Sacred and Profane Love Machine* was based on herself." Iris replied with considerable heat, explaining how she created fictional characters and describing the troubled history of her relations with Dame Rebecca:

I am surprised and upset to learn that V. Glendinning says in her biography that R. West believed SPLM was based on her family. You say "is this true?" If you mean did she believe this, yes. If you mean did I base the book on her family misfortunes, of course no! I knew, and indeed know, very little about Rebecca West's private life, and I have not read VG's book—and, needless to say, I do not base my stories upon other people's lives, or portray other people. I invent people and stories, and regard with horror the idea of exhibiting the adventures or misfortunes of real people in my fiction. To have done this to Rebecca West would have been a disgraceful and unkind act, of which I think anyone who knows me would know me to be incapable. Could you please tell me whether Glendinning's book implies that I did base the novel on RW's situation?

I had of course no notion that RW entertained this curious belief, and was puzzled by her coldness, even rudeness, to me at one or two parties. I was scarcely even acquainted with her, had never had a conversation with her, and this as it seemed gratuitous attitude surprised me. Then one day I got a letter from her

asking whether what she believed was the case, and saying that
from what she had heard about me & her impression of me she
had begun to doubt whether I had done this unkind thing. I wrote
back saying of course I was not portraying her family life of which
I knew nothing and hoped she would acquit me of any such rotten
act. She sent a very warm and friendly reply saying she believed
me and was sorry to have entertained such suspicions of me! . . .
It was [a] perfectly shocking thing to be accused of.

Iris deplored the culture wars going on in literature departments.
In October 1989 I told her about the Carlos Fuentes lecture I had just
heard at Boulder—thoroughly bogus but received with delight by his
audience. Urbane, upper-class, and American-educated, the Mexican
novelist followed the politically correct line and, straining to identify
himself with *la raza*, the common people, trashed the foundations of
European culture. She replied: "I note the (sad) anti-white-culture line
taken by C. F. This sort of ghetto sectionalism is so destructive."

Discussing the subject of college life, the sweeping social changes
we had seen and the greater freedoms students now enjoyed, Iris recalled how as a young woman, in the war and after, she had had important responsibilities. But on her return to academic life at Newnham
College in 1947–48, she was treated like a nun in a convent. When I said
I'd been having trouble with some young men in my classes, Iris, an experienced teacher, replied rather severely, "You must dominate those
students."

On another hot issue, the admission of men to women's colleges,
she sided with the Somerville students and opposed the current trend.
She believed that coeducation at Oxbridge was bad for women's colleges. The best female candidates were attracted to the glamour of
men's colleges and applied there instead, while few men wanted to
attend the women's colleges. She wrote: "Somerville, my old college,
[is] now in a state of turmoil because at last the governing body have
decided to admit MEN! A great storm is raging. The undergraduates
(junior common room) are, almost to a woman, absolutely opposed,
and the college is decked with big red posters and banners saying
NO! I am on their side. I enjoyed Somerville & St. Anne's life without
botheration by males, one could easily meet them anyway, the crea-
tures were all over the place. I fear however that economic reasoning
and the will of history will prevail!"

Her passionate support of women's rights—though not of feminism
and feminist criticism, which she considered "an insult to women"—

led to her criticism of the "benefits" of Islam: "That religion has, as well as its disregard for human life, another great advantage as it is the only creed which absolutely and fundamentally denies rights, even existence as human persons, to women! This must make it popular with the holders of power in innumerable countries!" She felt, however, a strong sympathy for India, rooted in her childhood reading and schoolgirl friendship at Badminton: "I have always felt connected with India & <u>love</u> being there (have only been twice). It's all connected with having read <u>Kim</u> when I was about 8. (And many times since.) And I was at school (progressive left wing boarding school) in England with Indira Gandhi, with whom I remain friends."

Iris liked Doris Lessing's first novel, *The Grass is Singing,* and felt she ought to read *The Golden Notebook.* But she disapproved of Lessing's turn to science fiction in *Shikasta* and her conversion to Islamic Sufism, which was antipathetic to women and insidiously connected to left-wing Arab nationalism. Like Lessing's early adherence to communism, Sufism may have been part of her search for an absolute doctrine.

Though Iris had spent her life in England, she was born in Dublin and could trace her Protestant ancestry back to the seventeenth century. She said she felt "completely Irish" and agonized over the sectarian violence on that unhappy island. In March 1993 she exclaimed: "About [President] Clinton . . . sending an envoy to Ulster to solve the Irish question! Our idiotic prime minister [John Major] seems to have allowed this to take place. The aim apparently is to study problems of 'abuse of human rights.' This is certainly surprising, as between two sovereign states! A visit to Dublin mentioning the IRA (not I think mentioned), might be more useful. . . . Our politicians are in total confusion, even chaos! Poor old Europe, poor old Russia, poor old Britain, poor old Ireland." She moved easily from contemporary politics to theological questions and also wrote: "I forgot to answer your important question. God created the world out of an uncontainable overflow of love. ('<u>Ebullitio</u>' [boiling up] is the word used by [the German mystic, Meister] Eckhart."

V

Over the years we met from time to time in London and Oxford (five times at her house, four times at mine). On the first of these occasions, December 1979, she and John came to lunch with me in Belsize Park, North London. I was teaching at the University of Kent that year, but we were living in Professor John Findlay's house, which I'd rented for the Christmas holidays. As usual, Iris and John arrived by tube rather than taxi, and I walked round the corner to meet them at the station. When I told her how well I'd worked that day, anticipating an afternoon with her, she jokingly remarked, "I *do* hope I'm not disturbing you." She was impressed that I was writing at the vast leather-topped desk and among the learned tomes, many of them in German, of that distinguished Hegelian, who'd held a chair of philosophy at the University of London. She knew Findlay's work and said that he claimed the nonexistence as well as the existence of God could be proved.

She also discoursed that afternoon on modern writers and academics. She had been reading Thomas Mann and greatly admired his major works, despite his obvious faults: encyclopedic material that was not well integrated into his novels and pedantic dialogues that went on too long. She asked what else she ought to read, confessing she couldn't face the *Joseph* tetralogy, and I suggested *Lotte in Weimar* and *Felix Krull*. She questioned me about Mann's life and exile, discussed Nigel Hamilton's *The Brothers Mann,* and spoke of Heinrich's sad eclipse in America.

John Carey, recently made professor of English at Oxford, she described as lively and hard-working (always a virtue with Iris), though somewhat rebarbative and known as Frosty John. She admired Frank Kermode's learning, but thought him a bit dour, like the Scots. When I said he came from the Isle of Man, she added that that was even worse, for their ancestors were all "elves or something." Asked if there was now a literary center in England where writers met to talk, she thought no such place existed. When I described my disappointment at the lack of social and intellectual life at the University of Kent, she was sympathetic to my plight and annoyed with my colleagues for not making more of the faculty exchange. John said it would be the same at Oxford, but Iris disagreed.

She asked about the centers of structuralism in America. I mentioned Yale, Hopkins, and Virginia, which published *New Literary History,* and we spoke of luxurious academic conferences held at the Rockefeller Study Center on Lake Como. She strongly believed (as I did) that structuralism and semiotics were harmful to both literature and literary criticism. She seemed receptive to my suggestion (supported by John) that she use her authority as a novelist and philosopher to write a critique of these theories and publish it in *Critical Inquiry,* a journal she found interesting. She felt there was a big hole in the center of the structuralists' thinking, that the Marxists did not feel obliged to use the same logical thought and clear language as bourgeois liberals.

She continued to travel extensively and in October 1979 spent a month in China, as a guest of the government, on a cultural exchange. (John had also been invited but couldn't go because he was teaching.) The group began in Peking, swung in a wide arc west and south, and finished up in Canton and Hong Kong. She was free to walk around and talk to students who approached her on the street and to anyone else who spoke English. China was still recovering from the cultural onslaught of the Gang of Four. English books were scarce and the food was terrible, though as guests they had the best available. There was very little to buy, but she was pleased to be wearing a soft blue hat she'd found there. Despite the puritanically restrictive social and sexual life, she was most impressed by the standard of living, employment, and education in China.

VI

Our next meeting took place in the summer of 1982. My wife, nine-year-old daughter, and I went to lunch with Iris and John at the house in Steeple Aston, near Oxford, where they had lived since their marriage in 1956. We arrived in a heavy rainstorm, making our way through the wildly overgrown—"we care for it ourselves"—front garden. The house was run-down and seemed oppressively damp and uncomfortable: furniture rickety, slipcovers stained, fire grate full of ashes, books and papers heaped on the staircase and floor. The walls had huge patches of green mold. The cold toilet, with its archaic thunderbox, was filled with language books and dictionaries, including Dutch and Esperanto. (In *Who's Who* Iris listed as her recreation "learning languages.") Iris and John did not go in for creature comforts, but lived in a kind of austere chaos. The car they drove, an old Renault, was as shabby and as much loved as the house. They kept bringing it in for repair so they could hang on to it, and had to install a metal plate in the front so their feet wouldn't fall through the floor. She laughed when I compared it to the paddle boats on the pond of the Boston Common.

It turned out to be a large party, and the other guests, an assortment of eccentric intellectuals who mumbled unfinished sentences, suggested that Iris was paying off her social debts in one gathering. They included Norah Smallwood, Iris's editor at Chatto; Gina, a young newswriter at the BBC whose father taught American literature at Hull; Peta Ady, a female economics don at St. Anne's; Iain McGilchrist, John's pet student—bright, disaffected, and precious, in pale linen suit and mauve socks—just completing a fellowship at All Souls and about to start a medical degree at Southampton; David Luke, an arrogant, bored, and decrepit German don at Christ Church; and Professor Chung, a rapacious Korean who monopolized Iris. Chung obviously thought he had reached the promised land. He pulled books off the shelves and insisted—despite her embarrassed reluctance—that she sign and give them to him. I thought she could hold her own or would resent it if I tried to intervene, and was sorry to see this greedy character take advantage of her kindness.

Looking like a convivial chemist, John concocted a potent brew of champagne cocktail—with bitters, Spanish brandy, and French cognac —that threatened to explode. Iris spent most of her time fending off the Korean and serving the plentiful food. We had cold chicken and tongue, risotto, salad and cheese, baked beans and olives, hard-boiled eggs with curry sauce. She said less than usual, but did mention that she was soon going to visit Stephen Spender in Provence. Though she planned to write there, she would not stay long because of the press of work. I carried the huge typescript of her latest novel, *The Philosopher's Pupil,* to her editor's car and we left at about four. Leading us through the wet fronds of the front garden, Iris seemed eager to clean up the gigantic mess (she had refused our help) and get back to her desk.

In October 1983—when I was back in Belsize Park, spending a grant year in London and writing a life of Hemingway—Iris came to dinner at our house. The three of us drank three bottles of wine, but the food was abundant and no one got drunk. We talked about her family background. Her father's people, she said, were lowland Scots farmers. Her mother's, the Richardsons (she was pleased to discover her connection to the Australian woman novelist Henry Handel Richardson) were squires who were given land in Ireland after Cromwell's victories. Her parents had left Ireland in 1920, a year after she was born, and the rest of her family was still there. Her father died in about 1963. She was devoted to her mother, now in her eighties, who suffered from Parkinson's disease and senile dementia. Iris came to London once a week to care for her mother, as well as for John's, and they rather dreaded Christmas with the two sick old mums. Just that day she had moved her mother out of a grim mental asylum and into a nursing home. But she feared that her mother, though much better off, would not be happy there or willing to remain.

Iris remarked that though she was a 100 percent Irish, she felt nothing but revulsion for Eire and couldn't go there. She disliked its backward education, lack of contraception, violation of women's rights, and fomenting of violence through hopeless promises of union. She had been a friend of the novelist Elizabeth Bowen and a guest at Bowen's Court. It was typical of the Irish government to break its promises and destroy the house as soon as they had bought it from her.

We talked of geniuses she had known or met. She observed that Bertrand Russell pretended to be a sage and moral guide, but actually behaved immorally and was "rather a cad." Wittgenstein, whom she knew slightly, had a strong, strange accent. But she did not take much notice of it because she was so busy concentrating on his conversation. He was a genius, impatient with small talk. Disturbed by his own homosexuality, he was also a devil who deliberately caused evil. He abandoned old friends, harshly criticized Jewish refugee-philosophers, told promising students to give up philosophy, and ruined many careers. She thought Elizabeth Dipple's recently published study of her work was competent, but said that Dipple didn't properly understand Wittgenstein and was quite mistaken in arguing that he provided the philosophical basis of her work.

Apart from Wittgenstein, the only other genius Iris had known was Elias Canetti. He was a good man who could have used his intellectual power, had he wished, for evil purposes. She knew and was impressed by John Searle, professor of philosophy at Berkeley, who had advanced J. L. Austin's ideas, but did not agree with his philosophical position. She did not have a television and was interested to hear about *Voices,* a program in which Searle had debated the mind–brain problem with Sir John Eccles. She thought she'd like to appear in that highbrow program.

Iris reflected that she'd been a writer since the age of nine and had always known it would be her vocation. Her first two books, given to her by her father and read at the age of eight, were *Kim* and *Treasure Island.* She still admired both of them. She read and reread classic novels, especially Turgenev, Tolstoy and Dostoyevsky, Jane Austen and Dickens, Proust and Mann. She'd been through their novels so often that she knew entire passages by heart and sometimes felt anxious that she'd "read all the books." She smiled knowingly when I quoted Mallarmé's *"La chair est triste, hélas! et j'ai lu tous les livres."*

Iris worked all day, and slacked off at night. She started a new novel as soon as she finished the old one. She was also engaged on a long philosophical work (*Metaphysics as a Guide to Morals,* 1992), based on her Gifford lectures at Edinburgh, which would take a long time to complete. She had no real models for her fictional characters, she said rather disingenuously, and warned that it would be pointless to try to trace their actual prototypes. They were all based on herself, "which I suppose is rather boring."

She wrote in longhand, making three complete drafts, the final one clear and typed by a professional. She'd found Carmen Callil too emotional to direct Chatto & Windus, and had no actively involved editor at Chatto. Later on, she said she was getting to like Callil, and thought her mixture of Australian and Lebanese blood was a potent combination. She sent in her novels and they published them as written. I amused her by quoting Disraeli's "When I want to read a book, I write one," and by comparing her to Bulwer-Lytton, who sent his novels directly to the printer and allowed the publisher to read them only after they were bound. A member of the Royal Society of Literature, she'd won the Booker Prize once, for *The Sea, The Sea* (1978), and thought neither Salman Rushdie nor anyone else should win it twice.

When I contrasted my intellectual isolation at the University of Colorado (where young people came to retire) with the life I led in London, she was surprised. She said she'd always thought of American towns as close to each other, because she simply got on a plane and flew on to the next place. Having spent her life in Oxford and London, it was hard for her to grasp the sense of remoteness one can experience in the American West.

Like Doris Lessing, Iris had been a communist in her youth. She knew some Russian, though not nearly as much as John, but it was not much help on her recent trip to Czechoslovakia. She had a close Czech friend and spoke of how dreadful it was for an intellectual to live there. He'd been imprisoned by the Nazis, and was later jailed by the communists for deviating from the party line. Unlike communists, who are in a dead end, many religious people, after abandoning belief in youth, rediscover it in old age.

She had surprised herself in the recent election by voting Tory for the first time; she had done so because of the extremely dangerous left wing of the Labour Party. She thought the disgraced cabinet minister Cecil Parkinson "shouldn't have messed about in the first place," but that it was very wrong of Sarah Keays, who'd become pregnant by him, to condemn him in public and ruin his career. Iris thought Keays would have been much better off by accruing sympathy as the injured party than by playing a vindictive role, which she would later regret.

In March 1984 we had dinner with Iris and John at their London flat in Cornwall Gardens, off the Gloucester Road. She had phoned to invite us on a Saturday morning. I was reading in bed, assumed the call was for my daughter, and let it ring. After about twelve rings a guest finally got out of bed and picked up the receiver. "I sensed you were at home," Iris told me. "I *willed* you to answer it." On the way to the flat, we came across a scene reminiscent of a Murdoch novel: a bedraggled assortment of tarty ladies' underwear, black and red, strewn across the damp pavement, together with a couple of crisp twenty-pound notes. Was this an acrimonious ejection or a hasty flight from a domineering lover? I scooped up the cash, but didn't mention this windfall to Iris, afraid that she'd somehow disapprove.

Their guests (more congenial than at the lunch in Oxford) included an elderly agent, Lady Avebury; a children's book publisher, Sebastian Walker; a young woman, Mary-Kay Wilmers, then on the staff (and now editor) of the *London Review of Books;* Robert and Shirley Lettwin, he teaching at the London School of Economics, she the author of a book on Trollope; and John Simopoulos, a Greek philosophy don at St. Catherine's (John's college), who reminisced, "I used to review for an important journal . . . but it packed up twenty years ago!"

The stairs up to the flat were steep, the rooms small, the kitchen rudimentary, and we felt grateful for the warm hospitality. The food was weird—and famously so. On their crowded table we had cold mackerel with lovage, chevril, and mayonnaise; two kinds of stew in watery gravy: one with frankfurters, one (John's ghastly specialty) with nettles; store-bought cakes; and many bottles of excellent twelve-year-old wines from the cellars of St. Cat's. Six of them were opened and served at the same time, which rather spoiled the effect. But this evening was not about fine dining. Iris and John were real bohemians— friendly and lively and talkative as ever.

Iris wore an odd, attractive outfit: black breeches and stockings, ruffled blouse and velvet jacket. She'd recently gained weight and looked a bit top-heavy. She didn't have much time to talk while entertaining eight guests, but told me she was terribly overworked. She was writing a philosophy book in the mornings and, as a rest from that labor, a novel in the afternoons. They were soon going to Berkeley, where John would give the Beckman lectures, and where I'd gone to graduate school and often visited during the holidays. But they were very vague about where and what sort of place it was, and unaware of its spectacular setting across the bay from San Francisco. They eagerly asked about places to see, and I whetted their appetite by describing the houses of Robert Louis Stevenson and Jack London, the Russian River and Napa Valley, Carmel and Monterey, Big Sur and the Hearst Castle at San Simeon. Later on, she recalled the wonderful asparagus and California wine they had in Berkeley. They stayed at the Women's Faculty Club on campus and were lulled to sleep by Strawberry Creek. Iris liked to quote her friend Richard Wollheim's remark that "Berkeley's the most wonderful place in the English-speaking world."

In August 1990 we met for lunch at our rented house in Islington. In the meantime we had done the *Paris Review* interview and had kept up the flow of letters. Iris had come to London that morning and had just been swimming. She'd visited the novelist Brigid Brophy, who had multiple sclerosis and could no longer write. She'd had a friendly argument with Brophy, who admired *Anna Karenina* but disliked *War and Peace.* When I mentioned we had been to see *Kean,* she said she didn't much like Sartre's plays, not even *No Exit,* and rarely went to the theater now except to see Shakespeare.

When her stage adaptation of *The Black Prince* opened in 1989, she wrote: "I am very anxious about the play, which contains a number of soliloquies and some literary theorising. It also abruptly mixes funniness and sadness." She later added that the theater was wrong for the play and the weather far too hot: "In spite of good notices I fear for it, however, since the London Underground is now frequently on strike, and this deters theater-goers!" Iris criticized the distortions and oversimplification of both the film of *A Severed Head* (adapted by Frederic Raphael) and the television adaptation of *The Bell.* She thought Ruth Jhabvala was lucky to have such talented colleagues, James Ivory and Ismail Merchant, who were so well attuned to her style and so able to convey it on film.

We also corresponded about the ups and downs of publishing. She became quite angry (revealing her essential naiveté about publishers) about the muddle surrounding the reprint of her first book: "a disgraceful firm called Harvester Press once published (republished) a book of mine on Sartre. The book was called Sartre: Romantic Rationalist. They produced a book entitled Sartre: Romantic Realist [1980]. On receiving a copy I pointed out this mistake. They apologised (vaguely), and I assumed they wd destroy all copies. They sold them all, and I'm now credited in some lists with two different books!" Since acquiring an energetic agent, Ed Victor, she'd made a great deal more money on her books—advances up to £50,000 for world rights. (Or was it UK rights only? She wasn't sure.) Before Victor (who'd recently invited her to lunch with the publishing tycoon Sy Newhouse) took over, she signed any contract put before her. The publishers, as they later admitted, had taken advantage of her.

Iris and John had moved in April 1986 from Cedar Lodge, the house in Steeple Aston, to Hamilton Road, North Oxford. As they got older, they found it too difficult to deal with the large house and garden, the lack of shops, the constant commute to and from Oxford. But after three and a half years in Hamilton Road, they became disturbed by the noise and by nearby "vandalizing elements." One weekend, without consulting her, John impulsively bought another place, and in the fall of 1989 they moved to a larger house in North Oxford, which they thought would have more room for their books.

We met at this house in July 1992, for the last time. John was retiring and had been moving in hundreds of books from his office at St. Cat's. There was not enough room for them and they were piled up everywhere. The front garden was overgrown—Iris was no good at employing people, she said, inside or out—but the back, which she tended herself, looked orderly. I brought along an article from that day's *Independent* about Cedar Lodge, which had been turned into a bed and breakfast hotel. Iris didn't want to look at the article and seemed pained by the idea. Ever on the move, she and John had just returned from a wet holiday in Cornwall, where they had rented a house and cooked for themselves, walked in the rain and read a lot of books. She was soon going to the country to stay with the widow of her illustrator, Reynolds Stone, and would then travel to Italy.

A. N. Wilson was working on her biography but hadn't got very far. She didn't know his publisher (which was Century-Hutchinson) and said he was also writing a novel. He had become involved with another woman and his marriage had broken up. Later, on she told me that Wilson had finally given up her biography to write one about Christ. Iris was "appalled" at the idea of having her biography written, yet felt it was inevitable and added, "I do rather hope this matter can be postponed until I have left the scene." But when Wilson finally abandoned the project, he was succeeded by Peter Conradi.

Iris's mop of hair was now wispy and gray, her complexion a bit blotchy, and some hairs sprouted on her upper lip. She wore an untidy smock, tucked her trousers into her socks, and walked with a sailor's rolling gait. We lunched in the same mediocre Italian restaurant, which I liked even less than last time (we agreed about most things, but not about food). She ordered a bottle of red wine and rapidly devoured a large meal. It was unnerving to see her concentrate on the food rather than the conversation. She seemed much less lively, curious, and responsive than usual; more unfocused, distracted, and withdrawn. Instead of lingering at the table, as we always did, she seemed to find conversation a burden and was eager to get home. In the car I said she was a precious cargo and asked her to fasten her seat belt. Smiling, she replied, "I'll risk it."

VII

In her last letters Iris began to complain of fatigue and of the great demands made upon her. She found it increasingly difficult to keep up with her correspondence and write her novels. I myself found it difficult to finish, or even start, her late fiction, which she faithfully sent me. Forced rather than fluent, her novels now seemed—with their convoluted plots, freakish characters, and bizarre sexual entanglements—a tedious reprise of her earlier work.

In November 1993 she wrote that she received about twenty letters a day and had trouble answering them, but did so out of a sense of duty: "I receive more & more letters asking me to do things, all sorts of people, all sorts of things. . . . A secretary alas is impossible—I could not bear it! . . . Oh never mind, one should not complain, there are many lonely folk who are desperately waiting for attention." That year she also began to express uncharacteristic complaints about the failure of her imaginative powers: "I am now very much at a loss, unable to conjure up any new scene. So I am a bit depressed." Later on, she repeated: "Of course I am trying to write a novel, but it is unusually difficult. Signs of age and time perhaps." Comparing herself to an acrobat, she added: "I am trying to begin another novel but cannot so far. (Perhaps it is time to stop juggling, and fall off the high wire. I hope not however!)"

In December 1994, I reviewed a biography of Anna Akhmatova, who seemed her kindred spirit, and tried to cheer Iris up by sending one of her poems. Addressing her lover, Akhmatova wrote that everything she had was for him: her prayer each day and her insomniac's fever, the fiery blue of her eyes and the white flock of her poems. In her penultimate letter Iris replied: "Many thanks for your lively letter and the lovely POEM! It is indeed a brilliant poem and I feel it close to my heart!" In her last letters she wrote: "Jeffrey dear, thank you so much for writing to me—with lots of love. Iris. . . . You are really super."

I loved and respected Iris, felt grateful for her praise and her friendship, sustained over seventeen years. I remembered that her mother had had senile dementia, felt something bad was happening, but didn't quite know what was wrong. I was deeply touched by her lonely need to go on writing, by her desperate struggle to retain her mental powers. Eventually, in February 1997 a report in the *New York Times* confirmed what I had feared: "Iris Murdoch, the 77-year-old British novelist, is suffering from Alzheimer's disease. . . . Ending months of speculation in the British literary world about her writer's block, Professor Bayley . . . said he first suspected something was wrong about two years ago when she failed to turn up for an appointment with friends. 'She had completely forgotten where she was going so decided to come home. It was so startling.'. . . Six months ago, she likened her so-called writer's block to being in 'a hard dark place' from which she was trying to escape." In a poignant letter sent toward the end of 1997, John described Iris as "deep in Alzheimer's now. All scans & medication etc. tried but nothing helps much, tho' she remains as sweet as ever. . . . But it's very rewarding to look after Iris, in a strange way, tho' nothing remains of the great creative mind, nothing." She died in February 1999, a few months after the publication of John's loving tribute, *Elegy for Iris*.

5

V. S. Naipaul

1932 born in Trinidad
1953 graduates from University College, Oxford
1961 *A House for Mr. Biswas*
1975 *Guerrillas*
1979 *A Bend in the River*
      now lives in Wiltshire

I

A writer arrives early at a cocktail party and the hostess says, "Ved Mehta's in there—go talk to him." He enters the living room and finds an Indian sitting by himself, staring into space. Remembering with some irritation that Mehta, though blind, is famous for minute descriptions of the people he's interviewed, the writer devises a pragmatic test. He sits unobtrusively next to him and waves his hand in front of Mehta's face. The man doesn't move. Getting more ambitious, he jabs two fingers toward the Indian's eyes. Not a flicker. In desperation the writer pulls out his ears and sticks out his tongue. For all his efforts, the Indian remains as still as a statue. So the writer gets up and strolls toward a new guest. With a self-satisfied air he points out the Indian, sitting impassively on the sofa, and announces in a confidential whisper, "You know, Ved Mehta really *is* blind!" To which the guest replies: "That's not Ved Mehta. It's V. S. Naipaul."

Naipaul's personality is enshrined in this story: his touchy, irritable pride; his aloof, secretive, hyperfastidious caution. He wouldn't deign to recognize the existence of the ass jabbing the air with his fingers, but if he did he would be devastating. By reputation he is unpredictable, bad-tempered, and cruel, with an acid tongue. A Trinidadian Indian, from a minority within an already marginal society, Naipaul is one of the greatest living writers. Like his predecessor, the deracinated Pole Joseph Conrad, he has taken possession of the language in hypnotic

74

prose and developed the master's great theme—the changes wrought by imperialism in the dark places of the earth.

In the sixties I did my doctoral thesis on novels of empire—Kipling, Forster, Conrad, Cary, Greene, and Achebe—and read Naipaul's books as they came out. His mind and art continued to fascinate me, and I thought it would be interesting to meet him. In the fall of 1983, when I was living in London and writing a life of Hemingway, I read that Naipaul was interested in the Irish patriot Roger Casement. So I left a copy of my book *A Fever at the Core: The Idealist in Politics,* which had a chapter on Casement, at his publishers and asked them to send it on to him. I spent the day working in the British Library, came home on the tube, and had a nap before dinner. I thought I was still dreaming when my wife rushed into the dark room to announce that V. S. Naipaul was on the phone. He had stopped at his publishers just after I left, picked up the book, and phoned to thank me that very afternoon. Friendly but guarded, he said he was glad to have the book, but couldn't meet me in the near future because he was just leaving on a "secret mission" for an English newspaper. Despite his air of mystery, it was clear that he was going to Grenada, which had just been invaded by the Americans, and his story duly appeared in the *Sunday Times Magazine* in February 1984. He asked me to send him my current and future books and, flattered by his interest, I did so.

In December 1985 I lectured on a cruise through the Caribbean, down the coast of South America, and along the Amazon. One of the books I discussed was Naipaul's novel *Guerrillas* (1975), which takes place on an island like Trinidad or Jamaica. I said that Naipaul described the postcolonial atmosphere: the squalid horror and racial hatred that lie just beneath the surface of a tropical paradise; the poverty, violence, and impossible-to-satisfy hopes of ordinary people; the betrayal by corrupt politicians who have replaced the colonial elite; and the hopeless, ultimately self-destructive ambitions of the guerrillas. I was enthusiastic about Naipaul, but since the heroine of the novel is raped, mutilated, murdered, and finally thrown into a septic tank, it was pretty strong stuff for elderly passengers on a pleasure cruise. When the ship stopped in closed-up Trinidad on Christmas Eve, most people were too frightened to disembark. But an officer was dispatched on a motor launch to fetch a priest and returned with an appropriately Graham Greene-ish character to celebrate midnight Mass.

Knowing that Naipaul liked to hide out and write in remote, attractive places, in early 1989 I suggested he come to Boulder. "In the mountains, there you feel free." He liked that quote from Eliot and phoned to say he was interested in the idea. But he warned me to keep his presence absolutely secret: I'd be the only one who knew he was there. Entering his elite conspiracy, I said he'd double the number of intelligent people in town. He laughed at that and told me to look for a suitable hideout. Certain he'd find fault with any place I found, I offered to put him up until he found a place for himself. But in May he decided against it. He wrote to say he'd been following my writings "with great interest," and that "Boulder sounds very far away and empty & nice; but perhaps no place is like that." He'd been on my trail, but I'd been unable to lure him to the Rockies.

Noting that Naipaul was inexplicably absent from the distinguished authors in the *Paris Review* "Writers at Work" series, I suggested his name to the editor, George Plimpton, who was enthusiastic. When I proposed this to Naipaul in September 1989, he promptly responded that he thought he was going to say yes to my request, which, he felt, would be more serious than the other interviews he'd given to journalists. I set about preparing for this interview, reading many of his books, all the previous interviews he'd given, and some critical books about him. I also compiled three pages of questions. But after the Murdoch débâcle, I'd decided I couldn't face working again with the *Paris Review*. I wrote to Naipaul about this and hoped he wouldn't be offended. In the meantime I did an essay on Conrad's influence on modern writers, which discussed Naipaul's *The Mimic Men*, his essay "Conrad's Darkness," and *A Bend in the River*.

In the spring of 1991, still flirting with the idea of coming to Boulder, Naipaul phoned from England to say he had to postpone his visit. More frank than before, he told me the *New York Review of Books* had commissioned him to report on Argentina. (I knew his long-term mistress there made the assignment more attractive.) On December 27, after I'd moved to Berkeley and sent him my latest biography, he wrote in friendly fashion that he liked my life of Conrad and had recommended it to Paul Theroux, who was writing a preface to *The Secret Agent* and needed this sort of book. He added that he hoped we could meet on my next visit to England. A few months later Theroux phoned unexpectedly from Hawaii, and we had a long, lively talk about Conrad and Naipaul. In January 1992 I reviewed Naipaul's latest book, *India: A Million Mutinies Now.* Though his three books on India had become progressively gentler and this one seemed to have lost its cutting edge, I was still fascinated by his complex relationship to the land of his ancestors, his attempt to free himself from the prison of his Indian past, and the ambitious scope of the book—to make sense of the great transformations in India from the Mutiny to independence in 1947 and on to the present.

II

Flattered by his hope that we could meet, I looked forward to my summer in London. I began to wonder if Naipaul was thinking, as I was, about his biography. He'd read several of my biographies and praised them, and knew that I took a serious interest in his work. Several people had told me that Naipaul was a veteran prima donna, apt to be charming one minute, brusque and indifferent the next. So through his agent Gillon Aitken (we still hadn't corresponded directly) I sent him my London phone number and waited for his response.

Going to see Naipaul in Wiltshire proved as circuitous as the route to the Holy Grail and, like an imperious magician, he devised a test. First, he called to say that I must go to Dillon's bookstore and buy an Ordnance Survey map of Salisbury (North), without which I couldn't possibly find his house. This seemed like overkill to me, since Lower Woodford, the village a few steps away from his house, was actually on my Shell Road Atlas. But I did his bidding, which amused me in a way, for he was behaving as mysteriously as people said he would. He then called again to give me precise and fussy directions to his isolated house, three miles north of Salisbury. At this point he disclosed his address and phone number, hitherto so secret that I thought I'd have to be met and driven there blindfolded. He warned me, however, *never* to use the number unless I was suddenly stricken with a dire disease or my car broke down en route.

Naipaul and his wife Pat came out to greet me when they heard my car in the driveway. His sad-wise face and hooded eyes were familiar from the photographs on his book jackets, yet seemed to have improved with age. His features were now sharper, more defined. He was sixty, yet his hair was jet black, not gray, and I wondered if it was dyed. Short, thin, and delicately built, as neat and immaculate as his orderly house, he wore a purple T-shirt under a striped dress shirt, silver-gray cord trousers, and white sneakers. Formal at first, he soon became friendly and congenial, and did not seem at all put out by the cancellation of the *Paris Review* interview.

We sat at first in the living room, where he'd been watching a cricket match between England and Pakistan on a large television set. He seemed especially keen on a South African–Indian cricketer, Mark

Rampra Das. I thought it strange of him to give part of his attention to the television, but put it down to Naipaul's well-known one-upmanship. "Are you interested in cricket?" he asked, with an obvious gleam in his eye. I said, no, I was actually more interested in talking to him. But he kept the set on all afternoon, glancing at it occasionally and explaining the snail-like progress of the game to me, using it as a distraction and making the process of seeing him more complicated. Would I put up with his rudeness or pretend to an interest I didn't have? This was, I thought, *his* Test Match.

He moved carefully, still recovering from an operation to remove bone spurs from his back. The surgeon, he said, had to "cut both muscle and bone." For someone who guarded his privacy so fiercely, Naipaul, fascinated by his surgery, talked freely about it. For a long time, he said, he couldn't bring himself to look at his scar. He thought it would be small and straight, but it was actually a long and slanted gash. The operation was a success and his pain alleviated, but he was still uncomfortable (especially when writing) and had to sit in a special chair. He also had to do some form of aerobic exercise and, like a prisoner, had worn a path by walking up and down his garden. His first serious operation made him aware of how much more he could do when he was young. He affected great weariness, wondered if he was finished as a writer, and feared he would suddenly dry up. He was anxious about the future—the loss of energy, the process of aging, illness, and death.

Despite the pain, however, he seemed to be in a good mood and enjoyed the conversation that jumped about from subject to subject. He frequently laughed (amazing!). He was even hospitable and encouraged me to stay to tea. When I mentioned that I'd recently eaten a *masala dosai* at the Vijay in North London, Naipaul—a vegetarian and teetotaler—praised the South Indian dish as an example of high art. He asked me about the house I was renting in Islington, and I told him about the fleas the family dog had left behind. Later that day, when I invited him to dinner in London, the fastidious Brahmin shuddered with horror at the idea of fleas.

Pat Naipaul—a thin, plain, pale Englishwoman—had large round spectacles and short white hair (a notable contrast to her husband's). The two had met at Oxford and were married in 1956. They had no children—Naipaul hated noise and anything else that interfered with his work. He was the constant focus of the household and her life. Evidently devoted and self-sacrificing, she seemed purposeful, yet sad. Pat said she'd wanted to invite me to lunch, but Vidia became so impatient and critical if the sandwiches weren't served exactly on time that she got "too frazzled" to have any guests. She was too shy to give me her homemade greengage jam for tea, so we ate shop-bought cakes instead. Warm and kind ("We feel we know you from all the books you sent"), she said she didn't help with Vidia's work, but was always there to take care of the daily tasks and provide much-needed emotional support. Thirty-five years of living with a dominant and ill-tempered genius had made her timid and watchful.

For many years the Naipauls had lived in a rented house on the Wiltshire estate of the reclusive aesthete Stephen Tennant, sometime lover of Siegfried Sassoon. After Tennant's death they tried to buy it, but found that the estate could not be divided. They bought this house in 1984—a fortunate move, as it turned out, because the new owner of the Tennant estate made many changes they disliked. Naipaul also complained about the ugly development in his own area. New housing increased traffic and used scarce water, but created no jobs for new residents. His house was tasteful and elegant, surrounded by chalky stone (good for his troublesome asthma). He slept in a single bed in his own room, which was decorated with Indian fabric and Indian miniatures. Their behavior seemed to confirm the rumors I'd heard that the sexual side of their marriage was over.

After the house tour, Naipaul suggested Pat walk me down to the River Avon, a few minutes away. He came out with us to the carefully tended garden and spotted a rare yellow-breasted bird, but couldn't identify it. Knowing I wanted to spend every moment with him, Pat tactfully urged him to come with us. But, afraid of slipping on the wet grass and hurting his back, he refused. I tried to question her about him during the walk, but she fended me off by saying, "You'll have to ask Vidia about that."

When we got back I was more interested than ever to hear about his current mood and ideas. Though he made some characteristically sharp, satiric comments, Naipaul was not, as I'd expected, gloomy or sad. He was close to his older sister in London, he said, but had very little social life in Wiltshire. He always traveled alone when researching his books. The Naipauls saw few plays and films, for he often got impatient with the performance and walked out. We got on to the subject of the Indian film director Satyajit Ray, whom he admired. Naipaul had once interviewed him and been told not to mention the director's work. But he soon discovered that was all Ray wanted to talk about. He'd recently had the opportunity to see him again, as he lay old and ill, but finally decided not to. Asked what I would have done, I replied that I'd interviewed several people on their deathbeds and learned some worthwhile things. I would have tried to see him, and left the final decision to Ray.

Naipaul was extremely dissatisfied with the English newspapers, a prominent feature of English cultural life. He now took the conservative *Telegraph,* but planned to stop it. The *Guardian,* he felt, was written for poor embittered intellectuals. Grossly exaggerating the fee, he claimed the *Independent* once paid Salman Rushdie £100,000 for an interview. Now it lacked the money to pay for good articles and had gone downhill. Though he studied the papers, he hadn't heard about the recent racial incident in London (Pat may have kept it from him) in which a group of skinheads had beaten a Pakistani to death. Both Naipauls mentioned the increasing number of murders in Britain.

England, he said, was "ruled by bandits of both parties who collude to ruin it." He was surprised—perhaps because he'd been reading only the *Telegraph*—when I told him that Bill Clinton was vastly superior to George Bush and would, if elected in November, improve American politics. We talked about the tedious obsession with political correctness, the severe thought control and fanatical indoctrination gripping American universities, and my decision to leave academic life. Because of current cant in the press, he observed, no black writer could be criticized and no blacks held responsible for the rioting, looting, violence, and murder in Los Angeles.

Naipaul got on to a frequent theme of his published interviews: the agony of writing. He wanted the world to know how much he suffered for his art and emphasized the effort it cost. Though the short winter days made things slightly easier, each page represented many hours of concentration. He thought and wrote so intensely all day long—in bed and in different rooms throughout the house—that he couldn't even read or write letters at night. *A House for Mr. Biswas* he considered his masterpiece. When he finally finished a book, he was so exhausted that he couldn't work for a whole year afterwards. Pat boldly contradicted him, pointing out that he used this time to write shorter pieces and plan his next book. When I mentioned the shocking plot of *Guerrillas,* he calmly said that in the Caribbean it was not unusual for white women who had slept with black men to be murdered.

We then moved on to every author's favorite subjects: editors, agents, and money. He called the much-admired Robert Gottlieb at Knopf "an accountant who didn't know how to read" (this was evidently Naipaulese for "didn't appreciate my work or pay me enough"), and added that Sonny Mehta, another big shot in that firm, didn't think

Naipaul knew how to write. Mehta actually tried to rewrite Naipaul's work and made him waste a great deal of time putting it back into its original form. Such editorial arrogance was quite common in my experience, though I was astonished to hear it could also happen to Naipaul.

I mentioned that I'd left my agent; he insisted that I needed one to get the best deal. He advised me to sell foreign rights for five years only, after which the rights would revert to the author and I could sell them again. (Nice idea, I thought, though I doubted if I could ever sell my books twice.) He was very interested in specific details about money and wanted to know how much my new Volvo cost, how my Conrad had sold, and how my friend Francis King managed to live on his writing. He told me to warn Francis, whose novel had been optioned by Merchant-Ivory, that "they don't pay." When I lamented that the publishers of Conrad had not sold paperback or foreign rights, despite the good reviews, Naipaul gave a priestly reply. The work was well done and would be rewarded in the future. Like a Kingsley Amis hero, I said, "I want it now!"

But Naipaul also had his eye on the great rewards. When I asked if he'd heard about the latest nominations for the Nobel Prize, for which he'd been repeatedly short-listed, he said he'd heard nothing and would not actively try to get it. He wanted to know, however, why Joseph Brodsky (who'd won the Nobel in 1987) got all the prizes and awards. I noted that Brodsky was an exile and the darling of the *New York Review of Books.* He countered, "So am I!"

I suggested that lobbying had been effective in the past and might even be essential. Thomas Mann helped Hermann Hesse get the Nobel, Roger Martin du Gard helped André Gide, Alexander Solzhenitsyn helped Heinrich Böll. (More recently Brodsky has helped Derek Walcott and Czeslaw Milosz helped Wislawa Szymborska.) I urged Naipaul, who certainly deserved it, to rouse his agent, publishers, writers' organizations in England, eminent authors and influential university professors, and especially his Swedish translator. He noted that his views were far from politically correct, but agreed that his Indian race, Caribbean birth, and the under-representation of English writers would help him.

It was clear that both Naipauls had actually read the books I'd sent them over the last decade. Becoming more expansive, Naipaul said that he admired the energy I revealed in my travels and my books. Perpetually exhausted himself, he'd expected me to look older and thinner, more intense and less relaxed. He'd just had a long, expensive, and tiring transatlantic phone talk with Paul Theroux, who'd praised my lives of Conrad and Poe.

I took this opportunity to make some advances of my own. I offered him the dedication of my biography of Scott Fitzgerald, and he accepted. He liked the idea, which I now put to him, of my editing and introducing his uncollected essays, but reserved his decision until he completed his current book, *A Way in the World* (eventually published in 1994). If poor health prevented him from finishing this book and fulfilling his contract with Knopf, he planned to give them a book of essays instead, but he thought this was unlikely and would let me know for sure in a few months. Now I took the Brahmin by the horns and asked him whether he'd allow me to do his biography. Yes, he was interested in the idea. He asked me if I had a good knowledge of his background, and I assured him I'd do whatever was necessary to master it. He also wanted to know if I could write the book without his permission. Yes, I said, I *could*. But since I needed access to his personal papers to do the book properly, I wouldn't attempt it without his consent.

That brought us, from Naipaul's point of view, to the most important topic. Test number three, and perhaps the real purpose of my visit, was how I could be useful to him. His poor health had made him think about the fate of his papers, and he was eager to move them to a secure place, protected from damage by fire or flood. In short, he wanted to sell his archive and asked if I could help. Having worked in the book department of Christie's and done research in many major libraries, this was right in my line. I offered to write on his behalf to three university libraries in America that I knew specialized in modern literature: Tulsa, Texas, and Yale. Tulsa had recently bought the archive of his publisher, André Deutsch, which included many of Naipaul's letters.

Pleased by this idea, he offered to show me his Holy of Holies, a collection of papers stored in a downstairs closet. Its key was whimsically hidden behind a book called *Those Wild West Indies*. Like a dealer in oriental curios, he slowly unveiled the precious stuff, as neat and well-organized as Naipaul himself. It was kept in fifty-four folio-sized boxes containing notes, drafts, typescripts, and proofs of all his books and essays from the beginning of his career to the present; letters he'd written to and recovered from his family; all the letters he'd received from other writers (including, presumably, my own); photographs of his family and of his numerous travels; tapes of him reading from his works in progress, which he listened to in order to rewrite. After the unveiling, he inscribed the five books I'd brought with me. We parted amicably and he promised to get in touch with me as soon as he had news to impart. I had lingered until late afternoon, and left with just enough time to make a dinner engagement in London.

III

The very next day I wrote to the three libraries (with a copy to him) announcing his desire to sell, describing the archive, and concluding: "I don't have to convince you of the importance of the collection—which will keep scholars and critics busy for the next hundred years—and of the extraordinary opportunity to add it to your library. I strongly believe, and have said in print, that Naipaul is the greatest living writer in English and is very likely to win the Nobel Prize. I urge you to act at once." They all responded immediately (though one of them referred rather amusingly to "Sir Naipaul"), but here my involvement ended. I had given each librarian the name of Gillon Aitken, who as Naipaul's agent took over the negotiations.

Soon after, Naipaul phoned to praise my speed and efficiency. He wanted to talk more about the biography idea, but wasn't sure if or when we could meet. I mentioned his interview with Andrew Robinson, which had just appeared in the *Independent on Sunday*, but he hadn't yet seen it. I also told him about the recent publication of an extremely negative book, Rob Nixon's *London Calling: V. S. Naipaul, Postcolonial Mandarin* (Oxford University Press, 1992). Naipaul's bleak, unsparing observations on the Third World had provoked several such ideological attacks, and it seemed useful to counter such writers with a book of original essays on his work. On a wave of enthusiasm I now proposed a third project—in addition to the collection of Naipaul's own essays and the biography. He seemed interested and asked me to send him a proposal. Though I had no relevant notes or books with me in London, I sent him a draft off the top of my head.

Two days later he called to ask me if I knew Bertram Rota Ltd., a book dealer who had offered to establish the value of his papers on behalf of the University of Texas. This seemed an odd question, since his agent would surely know one of the most eminent dealers in London, and Naipaul himself could hardly have lived in the world of letters without hearing the name. But I realized it was almost second nature for Naipaul to ask such *faux-naif* questions. He liked to cultivate an aura of remoteness, despite his detailed knowledge of how societies all over the world really functioned. Throwing me another bone, he praised me once again: "You said you'd write the letters, did so immediately and got fast results. That's the way I like things done."

He went on to tell me that the material he kept in Wiltshire all dated from *after* 1972. Twenty-seven more boxes, covering his early life, were safely stored in a London warehouse. We discussed where and how the valuation would be done. He'd just given a four-page lecture to Christie's for an auction to benefit the London Library, and this would help establish the market value of his work. He was planning a short book, *In My 25th Year,* about his first return to Trinidad in 1956, and wanted to reserve that material (later included in *A Way in the World*). He urged me to go ahead with the biography and promised to give me names of people to interview. He valued the truth and wanted the story to be told as fully as possible but, to avoid hurting others, said I would have to exercise discretion about his love affairs. He promised to keep me informed about the progress of the sale and to talk again before I left London, hinting that another visit to Wiltshire (complete with greengage jam) might just be possible.

Naipaul did arrange a second meeting, at his London flat, off the Brompton Road. On the fourth floor, modern, rather bare and clinically clean, furnished with Turkish kilims from Liberty's and some fine Hokusai prints, it had good views of the towers of the Natural History Museum, the Victoria and Albert, and the Brompton Oratory. Pat was there, but the presence of Gillon Aitken, a brusque, hard-nosed type who had come to look me over, made this a business meeting. Aitken began by talking about the sale of the archive. The Deutsch papers, he said, were sold in 1989 to Tulsa for $85,000. That collection included eighty-one letters from Naipaul, which made up about a third of the total and were therefore worth about $30,000. He thought he might get a million dollars (which I privately doubted) for Naipaul's archive.

Naipaul broke the ice by saying he'd been impressed by my energy and erudition, and had come up to London especially to see me. Aitken, I sensed, felt Naipaul had conceded too much by saying this. Though I knew quite well what he was doing, I enjoyed Naipaul's flattery. Impatient with the palaver, however, I pressed them for a decision on my three book proposals. Naipaul smiled benignly and Aitken followed suit. I had called the edition of Naipaul's uncollected essays *The Shadow of the Guru.* For this book Aitken would try to get 10 percent royalties for Naipaul plus 2½ percent for me, and I'd also receive a fifth of the advance. Naipaul noted that the collection would include his reviews of books by Christopher Isherwood, Edna O'Brien, and Francis King (he was very curious about my friendship with Francis, no doubt wondering what we said about him); his interviews with Graham Greene and David Hockney; and his reports on Grenada and the U.S. Republican Party Convention in 1984. He also said I might want to use some of the sixteen articles he wrote for the *Illustrated Weekly of India*. So this book was shaping up and I could visualize the work ahead.

Naipaul approved my projected collection of original essays on his work, which I called *The Achievement of V. S. Naipaul*. He liked my contributors and suggested adding Christopher Ricks to the list. I'd envisioned it as a university press book, but Aitken saw it as a trade book and thought he could get Knopf to publish it.

Finally we turned to the biography. Following my earlier discussions with Naipaul, I had drawn up an agreement that spelled out how I was to proceed, and both he and Aitken now said its terms were fair and reasonable. Naipaul would cooperate in answering questions about the facts of his life and would provide a list of people to interview. He'd grant exclusive use of his archive for three years and freedom to write the truth without censorship (taking particular care to respect the feelings of living people), as well as permission to xerox and quote from his published and unpublished works, manuscripts, and letters, and to reproduce photographs from the archive without payment. I left the agreement with them to sign and send on to me.

Business matters over, we talked about Naipaul's interest in Conrad. In 1980 he'd published with Sylvester & Orphanos in Los Angeles a letterpress, limited edition of three hundred copies, numbered and signed, of his own *Congo Diary*. The price was $100 and some copies were held back for future appreciation. The book had been plagiarized by Mirella Ricciardi in the American Express travelers' magazine, but he'd been compensated for the theft. He was about to publish in the *New York Review of Books* (December 16, 1992) an odd scholarly note on how Conrad had copied Flaubert in "The Return." We then got on to the question of why Conrad had married his uneducated but motherly wife, Jessie.

Naipaul said he no longer read contemporary novelists (Pat kept an eye on the competition), then commented on the merits of Walter Allen's novels and the "finely-textured prose" of another V. S.—Pritchett. He'd been reading the Revised Standard Version of the Bible, Josephus's *History of the Jewish War* ("imagine trying to describe a camel for someone who's never seen one"), and Richard Hakluyt on the West Indian voyages of Drake and Hawkins. Waiting for his back to heal, he had no travel plans of his own. He was reluctant to talk about his cur-

rent book, *A Way in the World,* which he hoped to finish by the following spring, but mentioned that many ideas in the first five pages flowed
into the book. He asked Pat to describe it, but as usual she said little.
He'd rejected several dubious offers for film and television adaptations
of his work, and none had ever been made.

He asked me about reviewing for the middlebrow *New York Times
Book Review,* and I told him how their irritating editors tried to soften
everything into blandness. Naipaul agreed that to write for them it was
necessary to have—hunching his shoulders and gesturing like a mon-
key—the "correct cringe." (I couldn't help noticing that Aitken, though
imperious with me, assumed the correct cringe with Vidia.) Chuckling
to himself, Naipaul told me that an Indian gentleman claiming to be
Naipaul (though presumably not Ved Mehta) had turned up at the *New
Yorker* offices, asked for money, and been given an advance, "Rather
humiliating, I suppose, if they really thought it was me."

IV

I returned to California at the end of August well pleased with what
I'd accomplished in London. I was writing a life of Scott Fitzgerald and
editing two paperback editions of his novels. But I needed to set up
new projects for the future, and these three books not only gave me a
corner in Naipaul studies, but were also immensely interesting. With
the help of friends and scholars all over the world, I immediately set
about searching for copies of Naipaul's fugitive essays. Many of them,
in Caribbean and Indian journals, were very hard to find. (Eventually I
published a complete checklist of 190 essays, stories, and reviews, and
55 interviews.)

I also sent him a three-page draft proposal for *The Achievement of
V. S. Naipaul,* which would include an interview with Naipaul, and a
complete bibliography of works by and criticism about him. My opening paragraph explained that the book aimed to

> provide for the first time a sophisticated analysis of all major as-
> pects of Naipaul's literary career and to lay the foundation of all
> future scholarship about him. It will consider Conrad's influence;
> Naipaul's literary connections with his younger brother, Shiva; his
> style and fictional form; his political views; his attitude toward
> colonialism, uneasy relations with the Third World, and explo-
> ration of recurrent ideas: identity, exile and isolation, dependence
> and loss, the absence of community, the sense of things falling

apart. The dominant theme of the book concerns Naipaul's analysis of cultural upheaval in civilizations as they change from instinctive and ritualized existence to historical weakness and vulnerability.

On October 5 Vidia (we had now progressed to first names) phoned me once again in Berkeley to continue our discussion of the questions I had raised in London and to offer some useful tips. He suggested I write to John Harrison, a friend of Francis King, who'd known Naipaul when he was seventeen and now lived in Madeira, and warned me—the careful reader of *Guerrillas*—to beware of corrupt Negro politicians when I did research in Trinidad. In a rare burst of enthusiasm, he said that his current novel was beginning to take fire.

He then went on to my collection of critical essays on him. Rather unconvincingly, I thought, for a writer who kept reworking variants of the same themes, he emphasized that every one of his books was different and that each one, whether fiction or nonfiction, was of equal importance in the total scheme of his work. I did not take this injunction entirely seriously, knowing his books varied in quality. Every author has tender feelings for his minor works.

Wanting, like most authors, to use every scrap of his writing, he urged me to include in *The Shadow of the Guru* his unpublished translation of the anonymous sixteenth-century Spanish romance *Lazarillo de Tormes* (which would sink the book), and alerted me to his three pieces in *Queen* (1961–63) that were not listed in the only published bibliography. Aitken did not have copies and Vidia's were in storage, so I'd have to find them myself. Most important of all, he'd sent two pages of notes on my proposal for *The Achievement of V. S. Naipaul* to Aitken. How typical, I thought, as I put down the phone. First Vidia phones me, then he phones Aitken and instructs him to send the notes to me. It was a characteristic example of what the military historian B. H. Liddell-Hart called "the strategy of indirect approach."

A week later, on October 11, he sent me a long, marvelous letter about my projected book of critical essays on his work, analyzing the background, themes, and unity of his books and justifying his method as traveler-and-interviewer. He wrote with the greatest diffidence, he said, since authors should not try to analyze their own books. They are unable to see them objectively and are not always aware of what they offer to readers.

He wrote, nevertheless, to make me aware of a basic concern of his books. His family was Hindu, and during his childhood in Trinidad they continued to follow their Indian peasant beliefs, habits, and instinctive life. Rejecting this background, Vidia had become an individualistic, self-critical, and self-aware sort of man. He thought that in the twentieth century most educated people, outside America and Europe, had developed in this way. His works, he felt, were more cultural than political.

India: A Million Mutinies Now had not anatomized the poor in India as Henry Mayhew had done for the London poor in the nineteenth century. It was not mainly about the life and work of impoverished Indians. It was, rather, about a country caught in a moment of cultural transformation: the radical change of an entire civilization. This book, which he believed to be his second best, tried to capture this crucial moment by portraying the experience of specific people. His inquiry was carefully developed; the people he met and described had to be typical of their own region. Once I understood that, and analyzed the major themes, the complex structure of this book, based on his carefully planned travels, would become quite clear.

This book about India, he insisted, was not political. Nor, as interviewers liked to ask, was it optimistic or pessimistic. It was about the tremendous cultural change taking place in a complex civilization. It tried to clarify that change in the course of an interesting narrative. The same thing was true of *Among the Believers,* his book about four Islamic countries. That was not a political book and did not criticize these countries. It was also about cultural transformation, a crucial moment of change in civilizations that were once remote.

This, he continued, was also a major theme in his early novel, *A House for Mr. Biswas,* which he wrote as a young man in his late twenties. In the difficult first part of that novel, he had tried to describe the strange, instinctive life of a community of peasants who had come from India to Trinidad and had only a vague idea of where they were. The chapter title "Pastoral" was both accurate and ironic. In the course of the book, the characters gain awareness of their situation. The theme of cultural change was also important in his book of narrative history, *The Loss of El Dorado.* When they invaded the New World, the Spaniards were still a medieval people. But they were transformed during the course of their adventure.

Vidia was pleased when a woman who worked in an Institute in Ahmedabad praised his accuracy, though he did not think an author's truthfulness was an unusual virtue. He believed a writer should always be truthful, and insisted that neither the Iranians nor anyone else ever claimed that he'd falsified information. He always wanted to report things as accurately as he could. That's why his books continue to live.

Since themes of cultural change and cultural identity reflected his family history and background, he always tried to look within himself. He saw no reason to rant about the evils of colonialism. No reason to beat a racial drum and attack one side or the other. Many other writers have done that. It was much better, and more rewarding, he thought, to look within. Simple critics, expressing current political beliefs, have searched for a political meaning in his books. That was both foolish and incorrect, and missed the point of what he'd attempted to do. It's difficult to explain this to interviewers, and he no longer tried to do so. Much better, he felt, to let the work stand on its own and reveal its own credentials and function. He had inherited the practice of looking inward from his father, who lived from 1906 to 1953. He recommended his father's collection of stories, *The Adventures of Gurudeva*, which had had a profound influence on his own work. In 1976 he wrote an extensive biographical and cultural preface to these stories, published by André Deutsch.

He insisted that his works, both fiction and nonfiction, were part of a unified whole. The nonfiction, he believed, should not be placed in a different category. During his writing career, he explained, he had used numerous methods and techniques to express his dominant theme. All these methods and techniques were important to him, because he considered himself a creator of appetizing works. He was not happy with the form of the novel, perhaps because he'd fully exploited it and now wanted to do different things. Since form and content are indivisible, new ideas need new forms. If he didn't try to do new things, he concluded, he could not continue to write.

Vidia's more specific two pages of notes on my proposal for *The Achievement of V. S. Naipaul* arrived, via Aitken, two days later. He emended the table of contents and drew my attention to perceptive reviews of his work by Gregory Rabassa and Karl Miller. He wanted a discussion of his techniques, and said that the writer is more than his meaning. Since authors have always been interested in the technique of writing, he felt it was important to discuss the technical aspect of his books as well as to analyze their meaning. He disliked my idea of replying to his critics and resisted the notion that his books were in any way polemical. His work, concerned with inner states of mind and being, not with political rights and wrongs, was above such debate. I might summarize the essays, he said, as I had suggested in my proposal. But he disliked the idea of answering the charges against him. Instead of discussing Naipaul's "relations with the Third World" in a polemical essay, he thought it would be better to write a critical essay on the value of his work as a history of his time.

I shared his view that his work was of a different, higher order. But I felt it had been attacked and interpreted in ways that hurt his readership and reputation, and for this reason thought a book of appreciative criticism would be useful. The problem (despite his use of the third-person "the writer") was that instead of merely giving his opinion and advice, he was trying to control the project. His statement that the final essays in the book "might be" as I had listed them suggested the role he had assumed.

The rest of the notes took issue with the way I had categorized *In a Free State* and *The Enigma of Arrival*. He understood that my proposal was written quickly and without my books. But he wanted to mention that I had omitted *The Mimic Men,* and he insisted (against all evidence) that *In a Free State* was not autobiographical. He strongly suggested that I revise my views to match his own before starting work on this project.

He also emphasized, in opposition to my view, that *The Enigma of Arrival* was not autobiographical, though he admitted that it had an autobiographical crust. He conceded that the fiction of Proust, Maugham, and most other writers also has an element of autobiography, but claimed that the reader is always aware of the real writer behind the mask. The major themes of *Enigma*—of change and movement, growing gardens, creation and decay—though enveloped by this crust, were actually fictional. It would be cheeky as well as wrong for an author to use real people to express his own philosophical views. The crust of autobiography defines the author, the seeing eye, and makes it perfectly clear that the eye portraying the oft-described English landscape is not actually English. The crust connects colonial England (manifest in the landscape) to the author's own colonial heritage. This makes the fiction seem both realistic and complete.

Responding to both his letter and the notes on October 20, I told him that the letter would be extremely helpful in revising the proposal for *The Achievement of V. S. Naipaul* and asked if I could use it as a preface to *The Shadow of the Guru.* The fiction versus autobiography issue, much more than a semantic quibble, was my fourth and most crucial test. I also realized that nothing could make me see *In a Free State* and *The Enigma of Arrival* as works of fiction. And Naipaul's assertion that they were fiction did not make them so. This was not his book, nor even entirely mine, for its contents would be written by the still undetermined contributors. I sent him a copy of my revised proposal, which I'd also sent out to twenty publishers. I kept his books in my original categories and concluded by reminding him that "this volume cannot assume final form until all the contributors indicate the approach they wish to take to your work." If Vidia was really writing with "the utmost diffidence," I thought, then he ought to allow the contributors (as I would, as editor) to express their own ideas.

Just as I finished this reply I received a letter from Francis King with a clipping from the London *Daily Telegraph*. "It has not been a good week" for Vidia, the *Telegraph* reported. He'd been "pipped to the Nobel Prize by his fellow Caribbean writer Derek Walcott," who'd once interviewed Vidia for the Trinidad *Sunday Guardian* and had now virtually knocked him out of the competition. But there was worse to come. On October 11, the day he sent me his long letter, he had "suffered another blow: many of his manuscripts, diaries, notebooks and letters have been accidentally destroyed at a London warehouse."

I later learned from his niece that the warehousemen, told to destroy boxes marked Chilean "Nitrate," instead trashed the ones marked "Naipaul." Aitken, hyping the market, told the *Telegraph* that the papers, about 30 percent of his archive, were worth "hundreds of thousands of pounds." But Vidia's English brother-in-law, a London lawyer, said that because of the warehouse's limited liability he wouldn't have much of a case against them. Vidia was devastated—friends feared he might have a nervous breakdown—not only by the stupidity of the warehouse employees and the cataclysmic loss, but also by the irony of it all. His papers were destroyed in London just as he was about to sell them, not only for money but to preserve them from fire and flood in Wiltshire.

V

On December 13 I sent Vidia another revised proposal for the collection of critical essays (with the categories unchanged); my published bibliography of his stories, essays, reviews, and interviews; and a tentative table of contents for the collection of his own writings, *The Shadow of the Guru*. As soon as he approved or revised the table of contents for the latter, I'd write the introduction, put the book together, and send it to Aitken.

That same day I started to do some work on Naipaul's biography by interviewing his thirty-year-old niece, Nisha Inalsingh, who lived in San Francisco. Attractive and lively, born in Trinidad, Nisha had come to Maryland at the age of four, grown up in Florida, and (apart from her exotic looks) was completely American. She had graduated from the University of Michigan, and worked for a year in an advertising agency in New York and in computer design in San Francisco. She was now studying for a business degree. All her cousins, she said, had gone to school in England or Ireland, and most had returned to Trinidad. Her last trip to the island was in 1989, when she'd enjoyed the food and the family's beach house.

Nisha told me something about the large Naipaul family. Vidia's father, Seepersad, had seven children (of whom five are alive): two sons, Vidia and Shiva, and five daughters. The oldest, Savi, married to an Indian Presbyterian, lived in Trinidad; Vidia, born in 1932, was next; Kamla, his sister, was closest to Vidia, who stayed with her when he visited Trinidad; Mira (Nisha's mother) was educated in England and had stayed with Vidia during her school holidays; Nella, who married an Englishman and had three children, lived in England. Suthi, another sister, had died in Trinidad in 1984 of a cerebral hemorrhage. Shiva, Vidia's younger brother, was usually gentle and soft-spoken, very different in temperament. But he could also be short-tempered and volatile, capable of exploding with anger. His *Love and Death in a Hot Country* suggested the causes of his unhappiness. A large man, overweight, melancholy, and troubled by constant comparisons to his more famous brother, Shiva drank a lot. He died of a heart attack in 1985 at the age of thirty-nine.

Vidia's liberal and progressive parents didn't interfere with the lives of their children and had no objection to their sons marrying English women. (Shiva also met his wife, Jenny, at Oxford.) Vidia's mother, a sweet-tempered, independent, and gossipy "busybody," managed a stone quarry. Widowed in 1953, she never remarried. Though crushed by the deaths of her son and daughter, she lived until 1990. *A House for Mr. Biswas* accurately portrayed their family life at Lion House (which still exists), and Nisha recognized the "pretty little baby" described in the novel as her mother.

Nisha gave me copies of the Trinidad *Sunday Guardian* of February 9 and 16, 1992, which reprinted two of Seepersad Naipaul's articles from June 1933. A *Guardian* reporter, Seepersad wrote that he'd been accused of vilifying the goddess Kali and threatened with death unless he sacrificed a goat in her honor. At first he refused to perform such acts of "ju-ju," but his fearful wife persuaded him to do so.

Vidia's favorite niece (he sometimes rudely ignored her siblings) saw him in both California and England. In San Francisco, wanting to impress her, he asked his host, "Are there any film people about?" Invited to dinner by Francis Ford Coppola, Vidia said to the *Star Wars* director, George Lucas: "Oh, you make science fiction? How amusing!" Nisha thought he really didn't know who Lucas was. But the producer who introduced them informed me that he'd told Naipaul about his fellow guests beforehand and that Vidia, pretending he hadn't heard of Lucas, was deliberately arrogant.

In England Naipaul proudly showed Nisha his garden and his Balinese shadow puppets, and took her for a walk along the river. They went into Salisbury to see the market, visit the cathedral, and have tea. He took her to London and, curious about what she found interesting, asked her, "Why do you like the city?" During her visit he stopped work and spent all his time with her, not because of family obligations, but because he was fond of her. Vidia would never do anything he didn't want to do, though he did say, "Be sure to tell your mother what we did."

Nisha had a good memory and a keen understanding of her uncle's character. Vidia disliked children, noise, and disturbance, and she couldn't imagine him as a father. Watchful and suspicious, he advised her to "be very careful who you associate with." Believing that Salman Rushdie's petition for support against the Ayatollah was a scam, that he was merely seeking publicity, Vidia refused to sign an appeal on his behalf. He told Nisha the goal of Moslems was "to kill people to gain a place in heaven."

Nisha thought Vidia could be funny as well as fierce, that many people loved him and thought him brilliant. But she never actually met his English friends and didn't think he was close to anyone. Though he wanted to appear independent, he was very pleased when friends did things for him. He didn't trust movie people, wouldn't work in Hollywood or sell film rights: his work was far too precious to waste on them. He was distraught by the loss of his papers, but would recover in order to carry on with his work—that was the most important thing.

VI

I enjoyed meeting Nisha, became absorbed in the biography, and plunged ahead with my work on Naipaul, unaware of the dangers ahead. In January 1993, however, all my elaborately constructed plans began to unravel. Vidia finally responded to my proposals through Aitken (we were back to that indirect arrangement), who delivered the first blow. All the uncollected essays from 1984 onward, Aitken announced, "will constitute, with one or two additions to come, the body of Vidia's next Collection of such pieces for commercial publication, and they could not therefore be included" in mine. Next, my proposal for *The Achievement of V. S. Naipaul* "does not appear to take account of Vidia's 'Notes' " and has "one or two anomalies": "*In a Free State* is a novel, not a work of Autobiography; and while Vidia would acknowledge that *The Enigma of Arrival* has 'an autobiographical crust,' he does view the book as essentially a work of fiction." *The Shadow of the Guru*, therefore, was postponed until after the publication of his next collection of essays. And Vidia would "ponder" the collection of essays about him. I began to see the wisdom of Sam Goldwyn's remark that "a verbal contract isn't worth the paper it's written on."

A few days later, angry and disgusted by their behavior, I replied that "Vidia specifically suggested I include his essays on Grenada and the Republican Convention (both 1984), so of course I included them. If you eliminate the nine essays published since 1983, you take away the best and most substantial works. And if he's planning to pre-empt my edited collection with his own collection of recent pieces, when could mine possibly appear?" I could only conclude that this project was off, and said so. In fact, Vidia's response to both essay collections, I wrote, was similar: "He encouraged me to go ahead" with *The Achievement of V. S. Naipaul*, "and do a considerable amount of work, and then told me to stop everything while he 'pondered.' I did not call *In a Free State* and *The Enigma of Arrival* autobiographies, but said they were 'autobiographical works.' In any case, I was merely writing a proposal to secure a contract. The contents would depend on what the contributors chose to write about."

By now I had acquired a different view of this project. I had submitted the proposal to twenty trade and university presses and no one was clamoring to publish it. Naipaul's stock in the academy was down and his commercial prospects poor. Despite the distinguished contributors and my experience as an editor, I could find only one publisher, St. Martin's Press, whose interest was lukewarm at best. St. Martin's originally offered a meager royalty and tiny advance—not even enough to pay the contributors $100 each. I had negotiated a better offer, but in exchange they wanted to specify exactly who the contributors would be, a condition I could not possibly fulfill. If some of them did not agree to write or failed to produce the promised essay, I'd lose the last half of the advance, lack the money to pay the contributors, and have a completed manuscript I could not place.

So, my letter to Aitken went on, "There's no point in doing this book

—especially if Vidia [still pondering] doesn't want it—unless I also do the biography." I had seen this book as a labor of love and offshoot of the biography, but it was now both a bone of contention and impossible to publish. Finally, I enclosed a copy of the same agreement I'd given Vidia in London and asked him to confirm that he still wanted me to write his life. I added that "though it would be an expensive book to write because of all the travel involved, my editor at HarperCollins said that he would not be able to pay me as much for a book on Naipaul as he had for Scott Fitzgerald." I wanted to let them know that literary greatness was one thing, commercial prospects another. Since I had left my teaching job, the advance was an important consideration.

A week later Aitken brazenly replied that "it was always clear to me, and felt it was made clear to you in my presence, that Vidia was intending to have another collection of his essays published on a commercial basis by his regular publisher." This was nonsense, of course, because if I'd known about their plans I'd never have dreamed of doing a rival collection. In fact, they'd never mentioned this book until after I'd left London. Aitken, Vidia's hitman, then went on slickly to tie *The Achievement of V. S. Naipaul* to the biography. He now twisted the connection so that the biography depended on the collection of criticism, rather than the other way round. Noting that I'd broken off negotiations with St. Martin's, he said he saw "that such a book would have little claim upon your time if you were not also to become Vidia's biographer. I have, of course, discussed your letter with Vidia, and he feels that we should not go forward with the biography at this time."

VII

In April 1993 the University of Tulsa announced that they'd acquired the surviving part of "the manuscripts, business and personal correspondence, and family memorabilia of author V. S. Naipaul." According to one reliable source, Vidia got about $630,000 in spaced payments and Aitken took a fat 10 percent. All I got was a volley of abuse the next time I ran into the curator of the Yale library. Furious at losing the papers to Tulsa, he accused me of double-dealing by contacting other libraries (though this is standard practice) to get rival bids.

A few days later the London *Independent on Sunday* announced: "V. S. Naipaul, casting around for a biographer, has fixed his eye on Ian Buruma, the Anglo-Dutch writer [and specialist in Asian history] who supplied the introduction to the latest paperback edition of his novel, *A House for Mr. Biswas*. . . . Naipaul does tend to want to control things.

The immediate question for Buruma is how far Britain's greatest living writer will allow his biography to roam through his private life. . . . The word here is that Naipaul intends to set no boundaries. He likes Buruma and Buruma likes him, even though he is reported to have occasional bouts of terror in Naipaul's presence."

I thought that Buruma was probably a decoy biographer, intended to keep other, more energetic ones at bay, though I couldn't tell whether he knew that's what he was. Five years later, in May 1998, Francis King wrote that he'd heard "Buruma was engaged on a book about Chinese dissidents and seemed to have cooled on the Naipaul idea. I think it is more likely that Naipaul has cooled." As of January 2000, none of the projects I proposed has been completed by anyone. There has been no *Paris Review* interview, no collection of Naipaul essays (by himself or an editor), no first-rate critical book about him, no sign of a biography, and he is still being fiercely condemned by postcolonial critics. The two books he's published in the last eight years, *A Way in the World* and *Beyond Belief,* have recycled familiar material—a return to Trinidad, a return to the four Moslem countries he'd written about in *Among the Believers*—and both received tepid reviews.

When I visited Paul Theroux at his Cape Cod house in July 1993, still "pondering" Vidia's behavior, I hoped he could enlighten me. Paul, his closest friend, had known him since 1966, when they both taught at Makerere University in Uganda. He'd written the first and still the best book about him, as well as two extremely perceptive memoirs, and had portrayed Vidia as S. Prasad in *My Secret History.*

Handsome, tanned, and fit after a trip to Martha's Vineyard in his kayak, Paul was a striking contrast to the neurasthenic Vidia. I asked him to interpret the recent chain of events. He said Vidia no doubt wanted to test whether I was serious or not, and finally decided that Buruma was more controllable. Buruma would never finish the book, he predicted. If he ever did, Vidia would never let him publish it. And after trying to deal with Vidia, he'd probably wind up in a mental asylum. Vidia, Paul said, had a long-time mistress called Margaret, who traveled back and forth between England and Argentina, where her family lived and where she worked as a literary agent. Buruma told Robert Silvers, editor of the *New York Review of Books,* that he wouldn't be able to mention Margaret in his biography. So much for Vidia setting "no boundaries."

Paul urged me to press on, despite the obstacles, with a biography of Naipaul. There were very few personal letters, he thought, apart from the ones Vidia had written to him (the Deutsch archive concerned only business matters) and the papers at Tulsa would produce few revelations. Having corresponded with Vidia, visited his homes, and met Pat, I had, Paul said, the "right understanding" to proceed. He thought that seeing Vidia and Pat was the modern equivalent of meeting Conrad and Jessie. Both authors were (or tried to be) "English" country gentlemen and had devoted wives who did everything for them. Both were hypochondriac, eccentric, conceited, and extremely touchy. Vidia also hated noise, and when RAF planes flew over his house he called the pilots "wogs" or "woggies"—the derogatory term for Indians. Again like Conrad, Vidia was fanatical about perfecting his work. He disliked the French translation of one of his books, and was proud to have forced Grasset to pulp it and do it again.

Paul was shrewd about his friendship with Vidia and the relationship of both authors to their agent. Gillon Aitken, Paul continued, had been managing director of the publisher Hamish Hamilton. When he became a literary agent, Paul was his first client, and Shiva Naipaul soon followed. Vidia saw they were doing well, and Paul advised him to join them. He did so and has prospered with Aitken. Though Paul earned much more than Vidia, Aitken neglected him, but "would attend, if required, to Vidia's toenails."

Much as he admired him, Paul felt he had to keep Vidia at arm's length. Perennially angry and embittered, Vidia never stopped complaining. He'd always refused to visit Paul on the Cape (where Aitken sometimes stayed) and, in any case, would be a terrible guest. He couldn't do anything for himself and—if Aitken wasn't there—would try to turn Paul into his houseboy. He would also be envious of this tangible evidence of Paul's greater wealth. Vidia said the lovely house, on top of a hill, with a fine view, swimming pool, and guest cottages, would make him sad. He'd think about all the mistakes he'd made in his life and wonder why he hadn't wound up, as he should have, in such a grand place.

Paul seemed in turn both fascinated and horrified by Vidia, and since this resembled my own feeling, I listened attentively. Whenever they talked, he said, Vidia spoke only about himself. *His* books were terribly important, Paul's were not. Vidia thought his own work was executed with a fine brush, while Paul's was done with a heavy-duty broom. Vidia was fearful that everyone, even old companions like Paul, was trying to exploit him. But he was an experienced and even outrageous exploiter himself, often inviting people down to Wiltshire so

that he could get a ride back to London. He worried about the fact
that friends he thought less talented, like Anthony Powell and Francis
Wyndham, were more financially successful than he was.

Naipaul never earned his advances and didn't give a damn. He
thought the publishers could wait and whistle for it: they'd get their investment back in thirty years. Yet he was always worried about money.
He'd left Deutsch for Heinemann to get a better deal, and was furious when the director of Deutsch, Tom Rosenthal, sold his letters to
Tulsa. Paul recalled Vidia saying on more than one occasion, with a
deliberate, calculating air: "I *think* I should like a million pounds. Yes,
that's precisely what I want." Yet even this symbolic sum would neither
soothe his ego nor bring contentment. At one time he actually expected
to get a cool million for the film rights to his novel, *Mr. Stone and the
Knights Companion* (with a screenplay by Paul Theroux).

Paul was amused by the darker side of Vidia's character. Naipaul
hated Salman Rushdie (who'd invaded his literary territory and could
write an excellent essay about him) and, for that matter, all other Moslems. He was fanatical about his privacy and particularly his telephone
number. When a high-ranking United Nations official once dared to
phone him, Vidia screamed: "Where did you get this number? You
must never call this number again!" He refused to talk to him and
slammed down the phone. In an Indian restaurant in London, Paul
saw him suddenly fix his attention on a hapless waiter. Staring hard
at the young man, he slowly but emphatically said: "*You* look like me.
I look like you. *I* resemble you. *You* resemble me. We are similar, indeed identical. We are the *same* person. Both of us, you and I, share *one*
single identity," until the victim fled in confusion. Domination and ma-
nipulation, that's his game, I thought, and not only with me. "Now you
understand," Paul told me, "why Vidia has no friends."

When my biography of Naipaul fell through several friends told
me that I was fortunate. I was reminded of this when, in a London
Times interview of May 11, 1998, Vidia manipulated the gullible reporter
and offered a self-serving revision of his past life. Now sporting a new
goatee and a new wife, he was described by the reporter as uniquely
original—"the only writer today in whom there are no echoes of influence"—even though (as he once acknowledged) he'd been profoundly
influenced by Dickens, Conrad, and Graham Greene. Emphasizing his
arduous struggle for recognition, Vidia claimed: "I never got any replies from job applications. The BBC laughed me out of court when I
asked for a little job in the talks department. The idea of a man like me
writing for the BBC—absurd!" In fact, after taking his degree at Oxford,

he was hired by the BBC and edited their "Caribbean Voices" program. Throughout the interview he never stopped whining. Yet he insisted (referring to himself, in his meek-humble manner, in the third person): "I'm not complaining, you must understand. The writer shouldn't complain."

When discussing my biography in 1992, Vidia directed me to exercise discretion, to take particular care to respect the feelings of living people. But in a *New Yorker* interview of May 23, 1994, he broke his own rule and described his frequent visits to whores, when he "became a big prostitute man." He explained that he did this to gain experience, to learn about "the act of seduction." Asked about this by the *Times* reporter, he said: "I didn't want Pat to read the piece. I thought I'd be able to keep it away from her." Pat of course soon found out about it and was deeply wounded. Though the *Times* reporter didn't question Vidia's odd reasoning, it's clear that there's no need to seduce a prostitute. The *New Yorker* revelation seemed to be Vidia's cruel way of publicly informing Pat, in the guise of disparaging himself, of her own sexual shortcomings.

Pat died in 1996. That year Vidia married Nadira Khannum Alvi, a journalist in her late thirties from Lahore, Pakistan. Though writers are often perverse (John Osborne particularly hated female journalists and drama critics: his fifth wife was both), it is extremely ironic that Vidia married a much-hated Moslem. Unlike Pat, always in the background of Naipaul's life, Nadira was very much present in the interview. She tried hard to refashion Naipaul the nasty into a warmhearted paterfamilias: " 'He discovered this wonderful fondness for children—at the age of 65! Children adore him too.' Naipaul nods approvingly." But this topic led her into unintentional absurdity: "So they are intending to have children? 'I don't have a uterus,' Nadira replies."

In May 1998 Paul wrote me: "I have just finished a book about Naipaul. I said I'd never do it, but I did. This is a secret for now." I knew Paul had a great deal to say, but wondered what gave him the impetus to write. A few weeks later the story behind the book made headlines in England: "Literary Lion Mauls His Mentor Naipaul." The *Sunday Times* of May 31 reported that the savage memoir, *Sir Vidia's Shadow,* "so fiercely condemns both Naipaul and his new wife . . . [that] Theroux's British publisher fears cuts may be necessary before it can be printed in this country."

The dispute began when Nadira sold some of Naipaul's books, including those Paul had inscribed to Vidia, to "make space for herself." Upset and insulted, Paul sent off an angry fax, which Nadira answered with equal force. She was a pushy new wife, taking possession of a literary idol as well as his household, and wanted much more than physical space. A battle of faxes ensued, as Vidia stood on the sidelines, pulling the strings and inciting his Moslem's warlike instincts. As their language became increasingly heated and venomous, Paul was prompted to vent the long-simmering rage that he'd expressed during our talk on Cape Cod. A friend who had read the book told the *Sunday Times:* "It is a very complex work. It does not shy away either from the debt he felt he owed Vidia, or the anger he feels about the past two years."

In a letter to me right after the dispute became public, Francis King shrewdly commented: "My view is that the [sale of Paul's books] was the occasion, not the reason, for the disenchantment. I think that Paul felt that, whereas he was so constantly laudatory about the work of VSN, VSN did not reciprocate." Another factor—the dissatisfaction both may feel with their career and reputation—might also have sparked the dispute: "Both men have, I think, produced excellent work in the past, but both have begun to run out of fuel—with the result that their later work, though technically as proficient as ever, tends to repeat itself."

In the *Times* interview Naipaul had announced he was secure, really "at home" in England, happy at last. My dealings with him left quite the opposite impression. Like many writers before him, including Dickens and Conrad, Naipaul had sought to disguise and revise his past, to reconcile his humble origins with his social and intellectual ambitions. Despite his arrogance and hauteur, his Booker Prize and knighthood, I suspected that Vidia still felt at times like an inferior outsider, a frail, unattractive black man from what he called "a ridiculous little island." My biography would have examined these old wounds, probing into the deepest beginnings of his art. It was right, perhaps, that he didn't allow that to happen.

At the same time, this deep sense of inferiority explained Vidia's need to assert his power, to dominate and control. I lacked the "correct cringe" he was used to getting from his wife, his agent, and nearly everybody else. In this test of wills, he held all the cards and I was bound to lose. When he couldn't dominate me, he torpedoed my projects and got rid of me. Though the experience was frustrating, it was not a waste of time. I met him and his first wife in their homes, and got to know him much better than most strangers ever could. I had many long telephone conversations with him, and he introduced me to Paul. He sent me some fascinating letters, which surprised Paul, who'd only received about thirty from him in thirty years. Vidia's letters showed an appreciation of my books and illuminated his own.

In retrospect, the man I met was not just a great writer, but a great manipulator, a great manager of his own reputation and public image. He thought he could order a biography as one might a publicity release, that a reputable literary scholar could be managed as easily as a Rupert Murdoch reporter. It would have been impossible, I realized, to publish his biography while he was alive. His essential traits—doubt, disbelief, scepticism, instinctive mistrust—he also inspired in me. Following his own motto—"Never give a person a second chance. If someone lets you down once, he'll do it again"—I broke off relations with him, and felt lucky to escape with my wits and integrity intact.

6

Francis King

I

Francis King's short biography of E. M. Forster impressed me with its inside knowledge of the subject's personal life and aroused my curiosity about its author. Unlike many English critics, King respected American scholarship. His review of my life of Wyndham Lewis in the *Sunday Telegraph* praised my "formidable powers of assimilation and organisation." So I felt emboldened to write him a letter about Forster, and his reply began our long-lasting friendship.

His letter mentioned our mutual friend Anthony Curtis, who'd been at Oxford with King and was now literary editor of the *Financial Times,* and said he'd read my *Homosexuality and Literature* and life of Katherine Mansfield. He explained that he had known Forster quite well through J. R. Ackerley, and provided the kind of personal information that made his conversation so fascinating: "I think that when D. H. Lawrence wrote that 'Forster sucks his dummy,' he was using a euphemism—and I don't mean for 'thumb'!" Always hospitable, he suggested we meet when I next came to London. I first met him in the summer of 1982, and began to see him frequently when I spent a year there in 1983–84.

As I came to know Francis, I learned more about his background.

A collateral descendant of the seventeenth-century bishop and poet Henry King, he was born in Adelboden, Switzerland, in 1923 and had three sisters. He spent his childhood in India (a major influence on his work), where his father served in the Indian Police and became deputy director of the Intelligence Bureau in India. His father died of tuberculosis, at the age of forty-five, in 1937. Francis won a scholarship to Shrewsbury, did agricultural work as a conscientious objector in World War II, and took his degree at Balliol in 1949. His literary career got off to a spectacular start when, still an undergraduate, he published his first three novels. He worked for the British Council in Italy, Greece, Egypt, Finland, and Japan from 1949 to 1963, and continued to write novels in his spare time. He then retired early, forfeiting his pension, in order to embrace the perilous life of a freelance writer. He was awarded an O.B.E. in 1979 and C.B.E. in 1986, and from 1976 to 1989 was a notably active president of PEN International. So far—as novelist, poet, biographer, travel writer, critic, editor, and translator— he's published forty-five serious books.

Generous and kind, Francis is also sharp, shrewd, and sometimes waspish. His friendships go back not only to Forster and Ackerley (whose *Diaries* he edited), but also to the novelists L. P. Hartley, Ivy Compton-Burnett, Elizabeth Taylor, and Olivia Manning. Through his work for PEN he knows everyone in the literary world, both in England and abroad, and has many amusing and often scandalous stories to tell about his contemporaries. He always seems at ease wherever he is. He has the novelist's intense curiosity and keen observation, and likes to watch the odd quirks of ordinary people in the street or on public transport.

Judging from photographs, Francis was very handsome in his youth and still was (at sixty, when I first met him) good-looking. He has a broad forehead, delicate features, and mischievous expression. He always dresses neatly and conservatively in a suit and tie, and has the air of a good little boy who expects—and will get—a treat. He loves chocolates and at one time rewarded himself with them when he worked particularly hard. This overindulgence gave him a pot belly and pear shape, but he soon pulled up his socks, lost weight, and returned to his normal figure. Though sensual and pleased with his septuagenarian sex life, he doesn't otherwise like to be touched. Disdaining the now fashionable male embrace, he always offers a cool, weak handshake—nothing more. But beneath his reserve is great personal warmth.

His house, just off Kensington Church Street, is small and comfortable, filled with good antiques and pictures. Several of the paintings were by the homosexual Bloomsbury artist Duncan Grant, whose work was reproduced on the jacket of Francis's *A Domestic Animal*. When he added a second bathroom and extended and glassed in the dining room, which looked out on the neatly tended garden, he admitted, "It is an extravagance, but I have no children . . . so what the hell?"

Though we come from very different backgrounds, Francis and I have the same high energy, volatile temperament, and ironic outlook, and share similar literary tastes. We both, for example, saw through the phoniness of an arty couple we met at a dinner party, and were equally amused by how Naipaul had manipulated an interviewer from the London *Times*. Like Paul Theroux, Francis has a fund of wicked anecdotes about Vidia's frequent temper tantrums and narcissistic behavior both in England and abroad.

Just old enough to be my father, Francis took a paternal interest in my career. He suggested biographical subjects, praised my work to editors and publishers, and engineered my election as Fellow of the Royal Society of Literature. One summer he also arranged for me to rent his sister's charming flat on Sidney Street in Chelsea.

In turn I tried to get his books published in America and to arrange a visiting professorship. I dedicated a book to Francis, and drew attention to the merits of his fiction in my reviews. Choosing his best novel, *Act of Darkness*, for My Book of the Year in the *Financial Times* in 1983, I said that "King writes with considerable style and wit, and provides the best description since Forster of the atmosphere and landscape of India. A disturbing undercurrent of evil swirls through the book and sucks most of the characters into an almost self-willed destruction." Reviewing his volume of stories *One Is a Wanderer* for the *Saturday Review* of June 1986, I described him as "a superb and subtle English writer who deserves to be better known in America" and praised the way he "seizes our attention by the variety of his characters and locales, the originality of his voice and the ingenuity of his design."

Francis and I regularly exchange our latest books, but I also admire his early novels, began to collect them, and eventually acquired almost every one. He signed and gave me some of them, and his sister Elizabeth, after some persuading, sold me her duplicates of some hard-to-find titles. She and I met in Sloane Square one misty afternoon, exchanging books for cash like two conspirators. When I lectured in London recently, I took along a sack of fifteen books for Francis to inscribe. I like searching out books written by friends and getting them signed, and they've forged a link between Francis and me.

He has a membership card to Kew and likes to take me for brisk walks along the Thames and past Syon House. We have lunch in the high-ceiled restaurant, stroll around the gardens (Francis, like God to Adam, naming the flowers and plants) and take the boat back to town. I especially like our all-day journeys when I don't have to share him with anyone else and can talk to him for hours on end. In the summer of 1992, when I picked up a new car in London, we drove down to Arundel in Sussex to see the castle and bookstores, have lunch, and take a walk around the town.

Four years later, we took a day trip to the Isle of Wight, where I saw a new aspect of his character—impulsive, even childlike. Since he'd been there many times, I put myself in his hands and was led around like a tame bear. He'd made no plans and, recklessly as it turned out, had us jump on the first bus we saw. We lunched at Carisbrooke Castle and managed to see Tennyson's house (now a hotel) at Freshwater. But a day like the one I imagined, which took in everything, would have required a hired car and meticulous planning. We spent so much time waiting for buses, which never ran on time and took circuitous routes, that we missed Queen Victoria's Osborne House, Swinburne's residence, Cowes, and everything else.

We had a lively dinner with Francis's old pal Neville Braybrooke, but had to leave very early to catch the last ferry. At Southampton there was no bus to meet us, so we hitched a ride (using Francis, in his linen jacket and panama hat, as a respectable front) to the train station. Once more the curse of English public transport descended upon us and we waited for several hours for what turned out to be the slowest possible train. Francis, impatient and jittery, distracted himself by buying several pounds' worth of useless stamped disks from a vending machine. We arrived at Waterloo just after the last tube had departed. Fuming by this time, I paid another £15 for a taxi home and swore never again to rely on British Rail. I was furious about the waste of time and money, while Francis, used to the system and far more relaxed and carefree, hardly minded at all.

During the fifteen years I've known him Francis has introduced me to many of his friends. A good cook, he serves roasts, chicken, and duck, with cheese and pastries. At his house I often met Joe Ackerley's half-sister Diana Petre, who looks remarkably like him. (Her sister, now dead, was the dowager Duchess of Westminster.) Diana took several long trips with Francis, sharing a house with him in Italy and India, until a careless taxi driver backed into her, shattering her leg and ending her travels. I also met one of John Huston's ex-wives; the author

Raleigh Trevelyan and his younger Spanish companion; the astringent and quarrelsome Irish novelist Julia O'Faolain; and the still tall and handsome John Lehmann, trying to fill a wineglass while trembling with Parkinson's disease. The weirdest guest was a rich, well-lacquered Japanese divorcée, in tight leather pants and ruffled blouse, who had hilarious designs on Francis—in her country, a living treasure.

Francis loved to recount the brazen adventures of a homosexual writer and politician with whom he traveled to Cuba. He'd disappear into a derelict building with one of his pickups and even have sex on the beach in the daytime—stunning and impressing Francis by his rashness. I could not stand one of his friends, the intensely mannered and affected editor Peter Day (Doris to his chums). He'd tried to prevent me from seeing the elderly Ida Baker when I was writing the biography of her sometime lover, Katherine Mansfield, and raised a great fuss when he found out I'd disobeyed his wishes and simply rung the doorbell of her cottage in the New Forest. Half my size, the feeble Day claimed he had pushed me out of his house, which Francis knew was absurd. Well aware of Day's delusions of grandeur, Francis remained sceptical about his fantasies, but found him a useful editor and friend and liked him anyway.

Conversely, he hated my friend, the writer Ian Hamilton, who'd savaged his autobiography, and couldn't understand why I liked the brute. Explaining the motives for the wounding vituperation, Francis said he'd heard that "Hamilton was once a half-good poet who was now a no-good poet and therefore embittered and envious. But my own explanation is a long memory. About twenty-five years ago, when I was on the Literature Panel of the Arts Council, I proposed a cut (subsequently implemented) in a grant given to a magazine [the *New Review*] which he was editing. Perhaps some chum of his on the panel—Karl Miller?—passed this on." Francis was always anxious about running into Hamilton at one of my dinner parties.

Generally, however, we like each other's friends. In 1984 he wrote: "I envy you your meeting with J. F. Powers. I have a great admiration for his work. Of American fiction writers he and [the homosexual novelist James] Purdy are tops for me, but most people over here have read neither." After an evening at my house, Francis noted the difference between the rough reputation and the sympathetic character of my close friend and tennis partner, the Australian writer Phillip Knightley—*Sunday Times* journalist, author of books on T. E. Lawrence and Kim Philby, and expert on espionage: "Someone once described Phillip Knightley to me as 'an intellectual thug,' but I thought that he was gentle and civilised and so much enjoyed meeting him. The one strange thing I did notice about him was the compulsive way in which he stuffed food into his mouth." The reason for this, I explained, was that Phillip not only enjoyed my wife's cooking, but also skipped lunch and was always starved by dinner time. Francis later wrote that Phillip's portrait, reproduced in the *Spectator,* "catches his quirkiness, intelligence and essential melancholy."

II

Francis would have made a wonderful father, and I regret that he hasn't passed his good genes on to the next generation. Though he isn't obviously homosexual and dislikes "show fags," he moves in gay circles, has male lovers, and is fascinated by inversion, which we often discuss. He thought a rather grotesque-looking young man we both knew pretended to be straight but was really gay, while I didn't agree. He was attracted to a young woman, whom I found too flat-chested and angular, because she reminded him of a boy, and theorized that for this reason bisexual men often married ephebic Asian women.

Francis's sex life was intriguingly complicated, and he wrote to me about it, usually answering letters on the day he received them, with an engaging frankness. When I first met him he'd been living for two decades with David Atkin, a much younger, sweet, and gentle actor, who frequently appeared on television. In September 1986, when my brother was ill with AIDS and often in hospital, Francis (without mentioning this disease, though I immediately guessed what it was) began to describe David's symptoms. We were strangely drawn together during those years by the suffering and impending death of our loved ones. Francis wrote:

> I know what you have been going through with your brother. . . . David fell desperately ill, with a high fever, over 40 for days on end, which no one has been able to diagnose, despite the interest of practically every specialist in Charing Cross Hospital. I have been going to the hospital every day for more than two weeks, and became more and more depressed when there was not the hoped-for improvement, but a steady deterioration. I really thought more than once: This is IT. Then three days ago the temperature began to fall. He still vomits if he tries to eat . . . and is therefore extremely thin and frail; but he is much more himself.

During the next two years, as David's decline ran parallel to my brother's, Francis sent increasingly grave bulletins:

David is in hospital having a massive blood-transfusion overnight. He looks ashen and now becomes breathless even climbing these few stairs. But he goes on working, getting up at 6.0 a.m. or even earlier. Very brave. . . .

   Poor David's health has yet further deteriorated. An operation, at first thought to be successful, failed to save the sight of one eye, and now he has only peripheral vision in the other. He has to go into hospital each day for "experimental" chemotherapy, which so far seems to be having no appreciable effect on his illness,

which still went unnamed.

   Finally, in May 1988, two years after the onset of illness, Francis announced that the ghastly end had come: "David died last Monday, after several weeks in hospital. He was so determined to live, trying two different kinds of chemotherapy, the second of which hastened his end, I am sure. He went totally blind, then lapsed into a merciful coma. . . . He was Japanese in the way in which, by a superhuman exertion of the will, he never once betrayed any panic or despair to me. After 20 years of companionship, I feel totally disorientated." As Leonardo da Vinci wrote: "The greater the sensibility, the greater the suffering— much suffering." Though I'd heard of similar cases, I never understood how David died of AIDS and Francis, his lover, was physically unaffected.

   At about the same time, Francis also had his own mysterious illness, originally diagnosed as a duodenal ulcer, and learned that health was always precarious, doctors chancy. Not until November 1988, six months after David died, did Francis discover the real nature of his disease. In a handwritten letter from the hospital he announced: "I've just had (last week) an operation for the cancer which has been causing me pain for a year. The specialist consulted ascribed the pain to duodenal ulcer, gave me pills, even gave me tranquilisers and anti-depressants! . . . What a hellish year!"

   David's death cut Francis loose from his emotional anchor and sent him into a sexual spin. David's role in his life was eventually filled, through an ad in a gay magazine, by Stanislaw, a pathologically secretive, fearful, and reclusive Polish dentist, whom I never met. He helped with the household duties, shopping, and cooking, and made his living by cleaning houses as thoroughly as he had once cleaned teeth. Dreamy, romantic, and impractical, the antithesis of the down-to-earth David, the Slavic-souled Stanislaw (Francis wrote) "is not always an easy character, but we have achieved a modus vivendi and I am really devoted to him (no longer sexually [as Stanislaw moved on to younger lovers]) and rely on him to look after the house and garden and, most important, me. It is not easy to find someone wholly efficient and reliable, intelligent and likeable." In January 1995 Stanislaw returned to Poland to be with his dying mother. Francis, after six years with him, once again felt bereft: "He is (unlike David) a far from sunny and easy character; but during these years with him I came to learn how it is that parents cherish 'difficult' children whom one would oneself heartily like to kick."

No longer Francis's lover and now back in Poland, he was still proprietorial. He decided that Francis must not employ a gay and found as his replacement a gawky, plain, and decidedly straight Burmese ("no cause for jealousy there!"), who was enrolled at the School of Oriental and African Studies. "The Burmese," Francis wrote, "is an intelligent, quiet, courteous youth, of good family, who behaves like an Oriental Jeeves ('In Burma we respect the very old,' he told me—I rather wish that he had left out the 'very')."

But unexpected problems soon developed with the vague young man we called (after Orwell's novel) Burmese Daze. He, too, suddenly became very ill. Francis feared he had AIDS and finally, having forced him to see his own doctor, learned that he had leukemia—which was almost as bad. Francis knew he could not take care of him for an extended period and, since the Burmese was supposed to look after him, didn't quite know what to do. He had no sexual feelings for the man, he said, "but I have really come to love him, in the way that one loves a brother," then offered a real insight about himself: "It is odd how all the most intense emotions of my life seem to have been crowded into the last twenty or so years."

As the Burmese languished and finally moved on to a flat provided by the council, Francis's emotions, which could be as romantic as a schoolboy's, soon became more intense than ever. Paul, a good-natured, tender-hearted car mechanic from New Zealand—handsome, butch, and gay—appeared on the scene. Paul told him that because he'd been physically and sexually abused in childhood by his father and older brother, he could only have sex with extremely old and feeble people who couldn't threaten him in any way. Wittily, Francis explained:

But when I made a pass, he declined sweetly, telling me that I was far too BIG and far too ENERGETIC for him. Apparently the old men have to be tiny and frail. So now, in a reversal of the situation in *Death in Venice*, I am aiming to achieve those requirements. . . .

Though I get no sex from him . . . these last weeks have been the happiest of my whole life. . . . For the first time in my experience the mere presence of another person can fill me with JOY.

Like Aschenbach in Mann's story, ironically enough, Francis loved Paul as an aesthetic rather than a sexual ideal.

During Paul's reign Francis went into hospital for a prostate operation. Put on a new drug that made it temporarily impossible to achieve an erection, let alone an orgasm, Francis complained to his doctor. This brusque and charmless man, in his early forties, rudely asked, "At your age, does that matter?" To which Francis replied that it mattered a great deal.

Meanwhile, Francis turned his sexual attention to a man from the North African littoral. An Algerian called Karim, he was so jealous that he assumed every friend was a lover. ("Really very sweet," Francis explained, when "not in a rage over some imagined infidelity.") Just then, to complicate matters, Stanislaw (who could earn more money as a cleaner in England than as a dentist in Poland) returned after his mother's death to live for a while—still invisible—in Francis's house. The master was amusing about the constant hostility between Stanislaw, with his paranoid fears and Slavic sulks (on his bed, face to the wall) and Karim (known to us as Kar-eem *brûlée*), with his wild gesticulations and Arabic explosions:

Unfortunately Karim is extremely jealous of Stanislaw, with no cause—we are no longer lovers, merely friends—so that I really have to keep them separate, S in the basement and K upstairs. K is really lost in this country—without either a residence permit or a work permit—but because of the Muslim fundamentalists, who have even assassinated known homosexuals, he does not wish to go home. He is a pathetic figure, with virtually no friends.

Francis found these jealous scenes quite stimulating and enjoyed having two handsome younger men compete for his favor. One day, after he and I had been to a matinée, he was extremely anxious about getting back in time to greet Karim, who came on weekends and had his own key. Francis wanted to hail a taxi, but I persuaded him to take a bus and we arrived home an hour before Karim turned up. Light-skinned, slim, and fit, he spoke scarcely any English. All his responses to my attempts to draw him out consisted of a drawling "Well, yes," or "Well, no." When I suggested he fill up his abundant spare time with a course in English, Francis replied that Karim had already taken one.

Ironically, Francis, the highly cultivated theater critic, spent his eve-
nings going to Rambo-type action movies—the only ones Karim liked
and understood. Karim—gentle, like all of Francis's lovers—was per-
secuted in his own country for being homosexual, and Francis helped
him when he was in a difficult situation.

In the midst of this emotional chaos, his beloved mother, a widow
for more than sixty years, reached her hundredth birthday. When she
was eighty years old, Francis had taken her to an Indian restaurant.
Vain about her fine appearance and eager for a bit of flattery, she asked
the waiter, "Young man, how old do you think I am?" "Madam," he
replied, "how am I knowing? Maybe nine-dee, maybe von hundred
. . . maybe more." "What an unpleasant young man," she remarked. "I
really don't think I like this place at all!" On another occasion, posing
for a magazine photograph with Francis for an article on writers and
their parents, she insisted on having her legs, no longer as slim as they
used to be, well covered. Now, her mind was still completely clear but,
nearly blind and deaf, she kept saying, "I want to die. Why can't I die?"
Her release came in 1993, her 103rd year:

> We were summoned to her bedside in the nursing home at 8.0. a.m.
> on Christmas Day, with the news that she had gone into a coma.
> With her amazing powers of recovery, she came out of the coma
> that same afternoon and began to talk lucidly. The following day
> was a terrible one for her and for us. She was struggling to breathe
> (pneumonia) and could no longer swallow. . . . Although I had
> been long prepared for her death, it came as a shock to me. I had
> thought her immortal!

III

Despite his romantic diversions, the greatest thing for Francis is his
work, and he's often remarked that "you and I must be the hardest-
working writers in the world." We both realized, however, that such
productive energy inevitably aroused the envy and irritation of reviewers, and made us suffer (as he put it) "from the number of books
we publish. Critics tend to be disdainful of any writer who rarely lets a
year pass without some publication! Yet Dickens, Balzac and even the
hugely fastidious James were even more prolific than we are." To which
he could have added Greene, Burgess, Murdoch, and many other modern writers.

I'd told Francis how much I admired the novels of his friend Olivia

Manning, who'd died in 1980, and how eager I was to write her biography. In 1982, soon after I first met him, Francis introduced me to Olivia's widower, Reggie Smith. Big, burly, and hearty—Guy Pringle of *The Balkan Trilogy*—he was infectiously friendly and talked like mad. We met at a pub near Lord's and Reggie organized a typically hectic schedule for the afternoon. Rushing from place to place, becoming later and later for each rendezvous, we never reached our final destination, tea with a mutual friend. I had to call to apologize, soothe her feelings, and explain that it was impossible to control Reggie or keep him on target. I'd never before known a real person who seemed to step out of the novel that so vividly portrayed him. The last time I saw him he was enthusiastically leading a group of American tourists down Keats Grove toward the poet's house, but he stopped to chat, turning his attention and brimming enthusiasm to me, until the tour group encircled us and gradually dragged him away.

Reggie told me that he'd been introduced to Olivia by his childhood friend in Birmingham, Walter Allen, who, like Olivia, was then reading scripts for MGM. Reggie borrowed a half-crown from her, and when he repaid it the next day he knew they would marry. They did so three weeks later, and he took her back to Rumania, where he was working for the British Council. He described her as *jolie laide*, with too long a nose but lovely eyes, skin, hair, and hands. Her father had been a naval officer in Portsmouth. She had miscarried a child and had no others, and put much of her maternal feeling into fighting for the humane treatment of animals. She was a close observer, had a near-photographic memory, and didn't need a diary or notebook. She did her letters, reviews, and housework in the mornings and, with these duties out of the way, set to work on her novels.

I was keen to set to work myself—on Olivia's life. But in 1985 Francis told me that Neville Braybrooke, coexecutor with him of Olivia's estate, "is talking of doing a biography, but I don't think that he has the stamina for all the research involved and his book would be more in the nature of a memoir." Since Neville held many of Olivia's personal papers and (with Francis) controlled the right to quote, I could only wait for the publication of his book. Though scheduled for 1989, it failed to cash in when *The Balkan Trilogy* was filmed for television and shown on *Masterpiece Theater*, and has still not appeared.

I was also increasingly curious about every aspect of Francis's work. When I asked which authors had been most important to him when he began as a writer, he replied that "Forster has had no influence on my short stories whatever. On the other hand Bunin, Maupassant, Maugham, Mansfield and Kipling taught me a lot." (One of his best stories, "A Scent of Mimosa," is about Katherine Mansfield.) As I stuck to my pen, yellow pads, and typewriter, Francis ventured into the maelstrom of computers—with predictable results: "Did I tell you that my new computer swallowed up 160 pages of my new novel—of which I had failed to make any print-out or copy? Two computer wizards diagnosed 'a virus' and then charged me £800 for rescuing what was lost—not in consecutive order but all jumbled up. I all but had a nervous breakdown!"

We often talked about why Francis's widely reviewed and much-admired novels did not, apart from *Act of Darkness,* reach a wider audience. I thought that both his overt and disguised homosexual novels were too restrained for gays and didn't give straights enough precise detail about homosexual lives. He depended in too many novels, I thought, on the same plotlines: an older foreign man picking up a good-looking young native in a Mediterranean country. His tendency to rhapsodize about muscular torsos and hairy male armpits turned off straights, and his emphasis on the repellent aspect of his characters tended to alienate the general reader. I wanted him to create more ambitious works and repeat the achievement of *Act of Darkness.* Francis replied: "I think that you are right about the earlier novels but not about the later. Unfortunately one gets stereotyped as . . . 'the writer who's so misanthropic.' Martin Amis is far more disgusted by his characters' appearances and behaviour and nonetheless sells widely."

His modest sales forced him into an arduous round of novels and stories, fiction and theater reviews, lectures at home and abroad, buoyed by the eternal hope (encouraged by options and followed inevitably by disappointment) that his work would be transformed into lucrative films and television programs. In September 1987 he wrote that what seemed to be a glamorous job had become, over the years, a kind of high-brow slavery: "I increasingly wish that I could give up the theatre-reviewing—the new arts editor, a cultivated ass, gets on my nerves, and in any case I weary of trekking out evening after evening—but my novels still do not make quite enough for me to feel that I can forego that monthly pittance!"

He did not give up theater reviewing, the best thing for him in the long run, until forced to do so by his cancer operation in November 1988. Francis's financial difficulties were partly relieved by an inheritance from David (including, since Francis didn't drive, the proceeds from the sale of David's Mercedes) as well as a small legacy from an elderly homosexual writer friend, C. B. H. Kitchin. But, money or not, he always entertained generously, spent freely, and seemed to live much better than his own income would strictly allow.

Though Francis has been publishing books since 1946, he is still keenly sensitive to criticism. In October 1993 he observed that his autobiography, *Yesterday Came Suddenly*, was "extremely painful to write—like performing a surgical operation on oneself without an anaesthetic! It was also nerve-racking to publish, since I knew that what would be under review [by Ian Hamilton and others] would be not so much my book as my character." In Japan, however, still revered from his time as a British Council representative and for books like *The Custom House* and *The Japanese Umbrella*, he is more appreciated than in his own country. In November 1994 he was delighted to have inspired a campy performance at the first gathering of his admirers:

> The only thing to cheer me at present is the foundation of a Francis King Society in Japan! Shusako Endo, who should have got the Nobel Prize instead of Oe, is a founder member. Quite weird. But also touching and pleasing. Apparently at the first meeting, an outrageous queen, with grey page-boy haircut and quantities of jewellery everywhere about him, mounted the stage and made a speech in eloquent praise of me. No one knew who he was! Perhaps a former lover of mine? Or perhaps a representative from the Kyoto chapter of Gay's the Word?

Francis was often invited back to Japan. During his PEN years and afterwards, he traveled around the world—with a Lawrencean compulsion to distract himself and escape whatever was troubling him—to endlessly boring literary conferences. In February 1992, for example, after returning from South Africa, he exhaustingly announced: "Other forthcoming trips are to Yugoslavia (Bled) for one literary congress and to Barcelona for another, and a tour of the British Isles by ship. Last year I travelled to France, Greece, the Soviet Union (as it then was), Korea, Austria and Poland! Too much." In Washington, he explained, "I kept asking myself what on earth I was doing there. It is really vanity that leads one to accept such invitations."

Francis took several disastrous trips—a Fawlty Towers–like cruise to the Ukraine and an intestinally agonizing jaunt to Mexico—with often dull, cantankerous, and all-too-feeble fellow travelers. Despite our friendship, the draw of warm winters, and the strong homosexual ambiance in San Francisco, I could never persuade him to come to California. When in 1986 I offered to pay his fare from Washington to San Francisco, he replied: "Of course I am not offended, indeed I am deeply touched. The problem, however, is not one of money but of *time*," for he couldn't leave his burdensome theater reviewing for long. He also liked more exotic locales and (just as he preferred the "difficult" Pole to more tractable companions) longed for " 'difficult' countries, where people are struggling to survive. They stimulate my creativity." He suggested we meet in Cuba, equidistant from San Francisco and London, but—despite the lure of visiting Hemingway's house—that decrepit, oppressive island didn't appeal to me.

Two of Francis's PEN conferences were memorable. In March 1986 I went to England to publicize my life of Hemingway, and Francis got me a ticket to hear Saul Bellow speak at the PEN Writers' Day. I admired Bellow's novels and was grateful for his responses to my queries about biographical subjects. He was the same age as the robust Arthur Miller; yet after another divorce, Bellow seemed not only jet-lagged, but aged and depressed. His rambling speech never came into focus and was a great disappointment. Afterwards, he offered to talk to me, during business hours at his publisher's office, about his friend John Berryman. Though I was keen to see him, my packed all-day publicity schedule, in and out of London, made it impossible.

Two years later Francis described the very different ways in which English and American writers engaged in political activity, and how the insensitive, impetuous Susan Sontag, on her own ego trip, destroyed a rare chance to free Korean authors who were languishing in jail:

> The Congress in Seoul was full of excitements of a rather disagreeable kind—mostly created by the American PEN Centre (New York) under the leadership of Susan Sontag. . . . She and her contingent arrived well in advance, to create a press furore about the four Korean writers in prison. The result of their strident demands was that the President refused to attend the opening ceremony and cancelled his party. I had been hoping for a meeting with him—similar to the 1-hour meeting which I had with the President of Taiwan—at which I was planning to ask him, in private, to declare an amnesty for the prisoners. But the American initiative destroyed that hope.

IV

Francis and I have talked, more than anything else, about contemporary—especially homosexual—writers. His comments about rivals often have a sharp edge. With W. H. Auden, Stephen Spender, Angus

Wilson, Doris Lessing, and Anthony Burgess, I had the opportunity to compare my own personal impressions with those of Francis, who knew them so much better. "I have known only three literary geniuses," he observed, "E. M. Forster, Harold Pinter and Ivy Compton-Burnett. William Golding? John Betjeman? Well, just possibly those two as well." I didn't share his enthusiasm for Ivy and Golding, thought Betjeman a good minor writer, and was surprised he didn't include Joe Ackerley and Olivia Manning.

My only memory of Auden, his wrinkled face looking (as he said) like a wedding cake left out in the rain, was his reading at Harvard in the spring of 1960. Slovenly, drunk, and rambling, he leaned over the lectern and pushed off his papers, which fluttered down to the audience like butterflies. Students rushed to retrieve them, though in jumbled form, and the reading continued more chaotically than ever. At that time, of course, I knew nothing about his private life. Francis "never felt that Auden really came to terms with his homosexuality, and that there was a strong element of masochism in the way in which he let [Chester] Kalman use—and abuse—him. Mind you, going to bed with Auden—who was always so grubby—cannot have been much fun." He also had a fascinating revelation about John Osborne, who collaborated with the Canadian actor-playwright Anthony Creighton on his early plays *Personal Enemy* and *Epitaph for George Dillon:* "He started adult life with a male lover, with whom he wrote his first play. He hated that and for that reason constantly railed against homosexuals—in a way in which no man entirely sure of his sexuality ever does."

The handsome, pink-faced, snowy-haired Stephen Spender had boosted my career in 1973 by including my article "D. H. Lawrence and Homosexuality" in his influential collection of essays on Lawrence. When I interviewed him for my life of Wyndham Lewis and asked, "Were you the model for Dan Boleyn in *The Apes of God?*" Spender charmingly replied: "He's a complete idiot. . . . But I suppose I am." In old age he still had, as Lewis wrote in that novel, the wide-eyed look of a startled antelope. Visiting Colorado in 1985, Spender, not at all jaded after a lifetime of questions, came to my seminar on Hemingway and spoke perceptively about his own visit to Spain during the Civil War.

I was therefore interested in writing Spender's biography and asked Francis to intercede on my behalf with his widow. He responded cautiously, stating that he might not be the best advocate: "Natasha [Spender] is terrified of revelations about Stephen's homosexual encounters. But these are common knowledge. Whenever he traveled abroad without her, he would find some male 'companion.' He even made little secret of being attracted to this or that young man in England."

Thinking, perhaps, of his own reputation, Francis also gave an acute account of why Spender, with his modest literary talents and embarrassing connection with the CIA-sponsored *Encounter*, had such a successful career and wound up with a knighthood. His long association with Auden and Isherwood greatly enhanced his reputation and, Francis added: "Stephen was a wittily entertaining companion, he supported a variety of good causes, and was adept at knowing the right people. He also lectured well and looked terrific right up to the end of his life. I suppose these things explain his position in the world of lit."

I'd encountered Angus Wilson—like Spender, tall, rosy-cheeked, white-haired, and knighted—at a dinner party in London. He held forth all evening, in the most delightful way, about his itinerant Christian Science childhood in seedy seaside hotels. He accepted my invitation, while in America, to lecture at Colorado. But one of my jealous colleagues offended him by trying to change the date we'd all agreed on and, to my great regret, he never came. Francis penetrated Wilson's jolly mask and revealed underneath a sad, insecure personality: "He is wonderfully invigorating company, but I suspect, indeed know, that, like many people who are that, he has a deep vein of melancholy in his character." After Wilson's death, Francis added: "He was a man who relied to a perilous extent on the approval of others. When the reviews became perfunctory or dismissive, he had no inner self-confidence to buoy him up and for the rest of his life was like a man slowly drowning."

In October 1971, after I'd reviewed *The Four-Gated City*, Doris Lessing invited me to visit her in Maida Vale. I'd always thought her a successful author and was surprised by her modest flat. Though heavy in her middle age (her large brassiere was drying in the bathroom), she was still an attractive woman. She praised Kurt Vonnegut himself as well as his lightweight novels (I later heard they'd been lovers). In retrospect, this seemed to mark the beginning of her descent into fantasy and science fiction, which nearly destroyed her reputation as a serious writer. Helping to carry the tea things into the kitchen, I clumsily dropped a cup and broke it. "I hope it wasn't very valuable," I said. "Actually, it was!" she replied in her straightforward way, and I thought it was time to leave. In 1987 Francis contrasted the two main speakers at a PEN conference: "Lessing is like a well-banked fire, cool on the outside and an intense heat at the centre. [The Israeli, Amos] Oz—who has grown arrogant with success—is like a firework display."

I spent an afternoon with Anthony Burgess in the spring of 1980, when I was teaching at the University of Kent and he was giving the T. S. Eliot lectures. A large, shambling man with wild, crinkly gray hair, combed forward like a Roman emperor's, he was a lively conversationalist. Like Francis Bacon, he took all human knowledge as his province, but also liked silly jokes. He told me one about Beethoven and his slovenly servant. When the master upbraided him, Karl replied tonally, prefiguring the opening notes of the Fifth Symphony: "What-can-I *doooo?*" That evening Burgess gave a brilliant talk, accompanying himself on the piano, on the different kinds of music in *The Waste Land.*

Despite the success of *A Clockwork Orange,* Burgess felt that he'd been penalized for being productive and hadn't got his due as a writer (his masterpiece, *Earthly Powers,* and his fine autobiographies had not yet appeared). He startled me with an acute but unexpected remark as we were walking around Canterbury Cathedral, seat of the primate of the Church of England: "This church, you know, belongs to *us!* It was built and consecrated as a Catholic Church, centuries before the Reformation, and to Catholics it still *is* one!"

Recalling the dramatic changes in Burgess during the years he'd known him, Francis felt that he had gone downhill after the death of his wife: "I liked him best . . . when he was leading a boozy and anarchic life with his first wife. Once that Italian wife [Liana] dominated him, I think that there was a decline in his character, as he became increasingly what she wanted him to be. He was so competitive, making derogatory remarks about Golding and Greene, and so grasping." He agreed with me that Burgess "was certainly, with Angus Wilson, the best lecturer I have ever heard; and there was no doubt of the *brilliance* of his novels and critical writings. But there was no real core to him."

Just as Francis was fascinated by the theme of appearance and reality in his fiction, so in life he tried to pierce the surface of personality to find the deeper individuality within. He emphasized the difference between the way Nadine Gordimer seemed to be and the way she really was: "There is a piquant contrast between the fragility of her appearance and the toughness of her character. Rather cold, no sense of humour. But admirable of course. . . . When she got the Nobel Prize [in 1991], the *Telegraph* rang me up for a quote. I said: 'Nadine Gordimer is like a pebble—small, hard and cold.' They did not use it! When I was in South Africa, even *black* writers told me how little they cared for her, telling me that she had used the racial struggle as a means for her own advancement."

Writing in March 1989 about Salman Rushdie's *The Satanic Verses,* which had provoked a death threat from the Iranian *ayatollahs,* Francis drew a neat parallel between a political and a literary war: "I only wish that Rushdie were a nicer man and his book a better one. It is like the Falklands. In that case we were fighting for an island most of us would not wish to visit; now we are fighting for a book most of us would not wish to read. A principle is involved."

Francis admired the mind and art of A. N. Wilson and reviewed books for the *Evening Standard* when Wilson was literary editor. Eager to know if Wilson was actually writing his on-and-off life of Iris Murdoch, I asked about the character of the author who'd found and then lost favor with his subject. Francis responded with a vivid sketch of a personality—like Gordimer's—that seemed mild but was actually quite fierce: "Whether A. N. Wilson is going ahead with the Iris biography I have still not been able to discover. She and John . . . disapproved of his behaviour to his first wife and two daughters. A. N. W. is a fascinating character. To meet him, he is like a caricature of one of those ageing, bachelor curates who get into trouble over choirboys. But he is not in the least homosexual, despite his liking for homosexual company, and he is tremendously tough, even ruthless under the pedantic, simpering manner."

We often discussed the two English writers who most interested me: Murdoch and Naipaul. As always, I counted on Francis for inside information about both of them. Iris and John were rumored to have a *mariage blanc,* and there were endless speculations about whom (if anyone) they slept with. In the early 1990s, Francis strongly denied, as Iris had, that their marriage was on the rocks: "I was amazed to learn that a friend of yours had told you that Iris and John were on the verge of divorce. Although I accept that common view that they have either never slept together or only did so at the outset of their relationship, their closeness to each other is never in any doubt. I cannot imagine either wearying of the other—much less either going off with someone else!"

As if to confirm my own uneasy feelings about Iris's recent strange behavior, Francis also noted that he didn't quite know what to make of it:

> I sat next to Iris at a dinner the other evening, when John Bayley was addressing PEN on the modern Russian novel. . . . She opened the conversation by asking me: 'Tell me, Francis, do you believe in God?' Having said that No, sadly, I couldn't, I then put the same question to her. She replied: 'I do not believe in God but I believe

in the idea of God.' After that, her conversation seemed to become more and more unfocused. . . .

She always used to tell me that (like me) she was never happier than when writing. But on this occasion, when I reminded her of this, she said: 'I am really only happy when I'm writing well.' I sensed that she had been bruised by the critical reception given to *The Green Knight*—which at best was grudging and at worst condemnatory.

Finally, in February 1997, after John's public announcement of her illness, Francis reported that "Alzheimer's had been diagnosed. Iris herself described it as similar to falling downstairs—you have one bump after another and with each bump become less and less in control of your mental processes. She has become childlike, according to the interviewer [in the *Times*], collecting stones and twigs. . . . It is all very tragic."

Unlike Iris, whose admirable character was essentially unaffected by literary fame, Naipaul, instead of becoming nicer as he reaped all the honors, became increasingly nasty. "He was not difficult at that period before he had achieved his international fame," Francis observed. "He has now become crochety and imperious and intensely misogynistic. . . . Everyone who has to 'handle' him complains of how difficult he has grown. The Caribbeans hate him because he is so contemptuous of them; and the feminists also hate him, for the same reason! . . . As you probably know, he was recently knighted. This can only be for services to literature and not (as in the case of Angus Wilson, V. S. Pritchett and Stephen Spender) in part at least for services to other writers, since of services to other writers he has been wholly innocent!"

He also took up the question, which had troubled my relations with Naipaul, of the genre of Naipaul's latest novel, *A Way in the World,* and of the frequent recycling and repetition of material that seemed to signal a decline in his career: "Did I tell you that I have reviewed the new Naipaul novel (so called)? It is an odd confection of history, fiction, autobiography, travel writing. Much of it is fascinating; but it is not one of his more successful books. He is a great writer, no doubt about that, but I have a feeling that he is running out of juice."

In June 1993, after the collapse of my Naipaul projects, Francis—who had often warned me to be wary—was unusually vehement. He sympathized with my disappointment and was sceptical about my successor: "I'm afraid that Naipaul is a *shit*—as well as being a great writer. His behaviour does not surprise me in the least. His character has de-

teriorated with fame, whereas Angus Wilson's improved. Ian Buruma
. . . writes well about Japan; but he is not a literary man and seems an
odd choice."

Francis is sometimes severe, though not unjust, about his contemporaries. Thus far, I've escaped whipping, as he seems to enjoy our
talk and correspondence as much I do. "I find both your letters and
your company full of amusing things—and always life-enhancing," he
wrote after our latest meeting in May 1998. "I get too little of that ener-
gising, entertaining, sometimes provocative conversation from most
of my [now elderly] friends—and none of it at all from Karim." The
companionship of an older, wiser man, not distracted by family and
children, who cherishes his friends, is precious indeed. Knowledge-
able, witty, and urbane, with fine manners and discriminating taste, he
writes highly polished letters that often make my day. In Francis I have
found an intimate friend. I can share and examine all experiences with
him, and always turn to him for help and advice.

7

J. F. Powers

1917 born in Illinois
1938 night classes at Northwestern University
1944 conscientious objector in World War II
1947 *Prince of Darkness*
1956 *The Presence of Grace*
1962 *Morte D'Urban:* wins National Book Award
1999 dies in Minnesota

I

J. F. Powers's fiction opened new worlds for me. I grew up in a Jewish family in New York. Though I had Catholic friends and girlfriends, their religion was foreign territory. I knew nothing of the Catholic priesthood, nothing of that social, emotional, and spiritual world. I spent two years at the University of Michigan, but could hardly claim to understand the rather bleak midwestern view of life. Powers's satiric stories took me into a particular world that I could never have penetrated by myself. Afterwards, on my travels, stopping for the night in a small town in the Upper Midwest, I'd notice a red-brick, lace-curtained rectory, its concrete steps clad in worn Astroturf, glistening in the rain, and I'd feel a shock of recognition. I could imagine the furniture, smell the polish, and visualize the priests sitting down to their dinner in the dusk. When I got to know several priests in Montana, they confirmed the truth of Powers's work. For twenty years I've taught his stories and novels, and often used them as touchstones. If I met someone who knew and admired his lucid, intelligent, and humane fiction, he was "one of us." If not, he desperately needed instruction.

Like the shy, self-effacing, and elusive Elizabeth Bishop, Powers published sparingly—only five books, separated by prolonged silence, during the last fifty years. His style, inspired by Joyce and Waugh rather than by American masters, is brilliant and witty. From *Dubliners* he learned to use concise description and poignant imagery to por-

122

tray the lives of obscure people who aspire to higher things (in all senses), but are caught in the net of the ordinary. Waugh taught him close observation, subtle wit, savage criticism of falsity. Powers, like Waugh, is deeply amused by his characters' faults, but at the same time conveys the urgent need—with salvation at stake—to rise above them. Like Joyce and Waugh, Powers assumes that the author shares the defects and aspirations of his characters.

Living and writing far from centers of cultural power, in Ireland and in Minnesota, remaining aloof from literary politics, refusing (in the flamboyant age of Mailer and Capote) to promote himself through readings and interviews, between books Powers is forgotten. As if to dare us not to read them, the titles of his last three books seem deliberately uninviting: *Morte D'Urban* (1962), *Look How the Fish Live* (1975), and *Wheat That Springeth Green* (1988). Every ten years he's had to be revived and rediscovered. I discovered the man in person quite by chance.

In May 1981 I was invited to lecture at the University of Minnesota. The English Department also arranged for me to talk at St. John's University and monastery, seventy-five miles northwest of the big city. I took a bus to St. Cloud, a small town set down among rolling farmland. It seemed as remote and empty as any place I had ever been. This impression was underlined by the clean-cut and well-mannered student, pleasantly fixed in a 1950s time warp, who drove me to Collegeville. I admired the peaceful sylvan setting, the pines reflected in the lake, the granite college, as well as the Mies van der Rohe chapel and the precious medieval crucifix on the altar. I also noticed a number of shabby priests, muttering to themselves as they stumbled around the lake. Austere as it was, the monastery provided a refuge from the occupational hazards of the priesthood: alcoholism, mental breakdowns, child abuse, and other scandals.

Jim Powers had been teaching creative writing (a term he disliked) at St. John's for many years. He came to my lecture that evening, we had a lively discussion, and he invited me back to his house. We hit it off immediately, drank and talked till late that night, and eventually became good friends. Tall, thin, and severe-looking, he was a handsome man with thick wavy hair combed straight back. He smoked a pipe in those days, and wore a sweater over his shirt and tie. He had a sharp Irish nose, thin upper lip, and features of clerical cut. Though often mistaken for a priest—because of his manner and his books—he was married and had five grown children. Later on, when I sent him photographs of a man who bore a striking resemblance to him, he seemed annoyed by the living look-alike—as Moslems are when you snatch their image with a camera—and wrote, "[I'm] returning the photos of your neighbor who I must say is even handsomer than me." After midnight, I left his house and walked past the dark pines and under the clear, starry sky. Pondering the contrast between Jim's conviviality and the chilly isolation of rural Minnesota, I went to sleep, for the first time in my life, in a monastic cell.

Between 1981 and 1998 Jim wrote me sixty letters, inscribed many editions of his books, commented on the short story I sent him and my essay on his work, and sent blurbs for my biographies of Hemingway and Fitzgerald. I also took notes on three other visits to Collegeville (Jim rarely went anywhere). This material illuminates his life, character, work, ideas, and beliefs.

II

Jim lived among Catholics and divided the world into those who were Catholic and Catholic writers (Evelyn Waugh and Flannery O'Connor), and those who were not. The first counted in the most important way; the others, sadly deluded and lacking the Faith, usually did not. Edmund Wilson, for example, so unaware of religion, was not (Jim felt) very intelligent. We came from very different backgrounds and he was old enough to be my father; but his sons were nonachievers, living in Ireland and partly supported by Jim, and our filial bond was strong. We both loved literary gossip, valued wit, and took a satiric view of human folly.

I could not share his enthusiasm for the provincial Irish authors Frank O'Connor and Sean O'Faolain and for the tame Americans Katherine Anne Porter and Peter Taylor, all of whom he had known. Nor was he terribly keen on my favorite authors: Thomas Mann, Wyndham Lewis, D. H. Lawrence, Malraux, and Hemingway. I persuaded him to read Lewis's *The Revenge for Love;* and I was always surprised by the books, so crucial to my own literary experience, that—in his deliberately restricted universe—he *hadn't* read: *The Magic Mountain* and *Doctor Faustus, Lady Chatterley's Lover, Man's Fate,* and *For Whom the Bell Tolls.* But we both loved Joyce and Fitzgerald, Bishop and Bellow, Roethke and Lowell.

Early on Jim defined our friendship by creating wildly exaggerated, semi-comic characters for the two of us: believer–atheist, corny midwesterner–savvy easterner, ignorant autodidact–learned professor, cautious introvert–reckless wild man, blocked writer–prodigious inkspiller, hoary hermit–social butterfly, resolute recluse–manic traveler.

He liked to make fun of my frantic journeys: "As is now usual," he wrote, "I found your activity and itinerary, just reading about it, exhausting. . . . Do you, at the start of your transatlantic flights, call for the plane's carpenter and have him knock up a desk for you, like Trollope?"

We certainly had very different approaches to the act of writing itself. I never found out exactly what Jim did in his office. But it seemed, from his snail-like progress (or lack of it) that he very carefully wrote one or two sentences in the morning and then, dissatisfied with what he'd done, slowly crossed them out in the afternoon. Jim, for his part, pretended to be puzzled by my apparently endless outpouring of books and articles: "You must be the most Napoleonic of writers, in the sense that you are constantly on the move, beginning and finishing books at an amazing rate, and very good books too." But, always taking the long view, he slyly warned me, "Hell for you would be writer's block, so watch yourself here below lest that be your eternal lot."

I was full of suggestions, plans and projects *for him*. These he invariably rejected. Trying to pry him out of his arctic fastness (at St. John's in the winter there was only a barbed-wire fence between him and the North Pole) and believing an escape from his monastic existence would jump-start his writing, I invited him to meet me in the warmth of Florida or California, to lecture in Colorado, or to read at an Alabama writers' conference. To which he replied, "Thank you for the invitation to visit Key West: had you suggested Tibet, it wouldn't have been any funnier." Grasping at straws, I offered to meet him outside the Potala palace in Lhasa on Christmas Day.

Disappointed, sometimes with himself and always with publishers, he was surprised when I managed to extract a substantial sum for British rights of my *Hemingway:* "I am floored by the Macmillan advance; no more than you deserve; but that is what floors me, that you may be getting what you deserve." Eager to give him what he deserved, I wanted to organize a special issue of *Modern Fiction Studies* devoted to his work, interview him for the *Paris Review,* edit a collection of his essays, get his books back into print in America. All in vain. He did not object to my writing an introduction to his fiction in a series called Understanding Contemporary American Literature, but that project also fell through. The University of South Carolina Press first offered me a minuscule advance and promised 10 percent royalties on list price. When they quietly reduced this to only 6 percent and insisted that "a higher royalty would cause us economic difficulties," I bailed out.

Jim's life was governed by scruples, which sometimes tormented him. When I asked if I could dedicate my life of D. H. Lawrence to him, he replied, "I'm not a Lawrence man, you know, and would feel odd, somehow, would be afraid, assuming anyone recognized my name, that I might seem to be passing as such." Some years later he finally accepted a dedication—though not without the usual conscientious qualifications: "about the Conrad book, I am flattered, naturally, and do, or did in the 50s, have some interest in his work, but wish you'd choose someone more deserving: meaning I don't feel right for the honor. Does this mean I'm declining or rejecting it? No, it just means what I say, and is *not* humility."

Unlike many slow or blocked writers, Jim was not at all resentful or jealous of worldly success and seemed genuinely pleased by mine. His blurbs for my books on Hemingway (1985) and Fitzgerald (1994) were thoughtful and elegantly expressed, valuable précis of their character and careers, little works of art in themselves. He called Hemingway "the famous performer who acted from the All-American hope that what goes up may *not* come down, but did, in this case, tragically."

Jim rated Fitzgerald above Hemingway and Faulkner; felt "Absolution" was important to him; and (a loyal Minnesotan) said his favorite, "knockout" story was "Winter Dreams." Fitzgerald's negative portrayal of a Germanic priest from the Upper Midwest in "Absolution" and of Judy Jones's wild golf ball that strikes another player in "Winter Dreams" reappeared in Powers's novel *Morte D'Urban*. So his comment on Fitzgerald was a labor of love. He emphasized the "admiration, love and mercy [that] Fitzgerald himself showed for others in his life—Hemingway, Zelda, Lardner—and himself deserved even more."

On my first visit to Jim in 1984, three years after my lecture at St. John's, I started to tell him about my last, poignant meeting with the English writer Gerald Brenan and asked how, technically, he would transform this encounter into a short story. Alarmed by my question, he cut me off and said the weather was too warm to discuss it. I already knew how to write it, he disingenuously claimed, and should just tell it as it happened. Puzzled by his uncharacteristically curt response, I didn't know whether he thought I might lose it by talking about it or whether he didn't like to discuss his art and give away trade secrets.

Three months later I sent him the seven-page story I had written about Gerald Brenan. As a young man in the 1920s, Gerald, a friend of Virginia and Leonard Woolf, had pursued the Bloomsbury painter Carrington, the great love of his life. When he finally got her into bed, she lit a cigarette to show her impatience and boredom. Uneducated and impoverished, he broke with her and set off for southern Spain where he could live cheaply and educate himself. He became a first-rate travel writer, memoirist, and historian of modern Spain, and to my delight he was very much alive and living nearby when I went to live in Spain in 1971. My story took place near the end of his life, when I visited him in a London nursing home.

As if to make amends for his unwillingness to help, Jim made extensive annotations (improving the text every time) and added two pages of handwritten comments. They revealed his way of achieving the greatest effect and showed, with tactful modesty, his brilliant method of teaching:

Jeffrey: <u>At this point</u> [page 2] I think: he gallops along, isn't good at the MOMENT (the little still-life shots) and maybe doesn't want to be. Writes more like a novelist or the good biographer he is. Gets on with it. A short story goes slow—a novel fast. I enjoyed ". . . and [his lover] asked him—if he was finished—to get off." But it sticks out, like a joke, isn't rendered as it perhaps should be in a short story—and is that the end of the "nymph"? Just in there to show he's a romanticist? . . . I may be wrong about this. What I'm trying to say is that your writing isn't right, close <u>enough</u>. . . . BUT I WON'T DO ANY MORE.

Caught up in the pedagogical exercise and wanting to give me the benefit of his experience, he continued to correct and comment on the story:

LATER: Sorry, I did.
    I don't think so, Jeffrey. Your heart's in the right place. But that's not enough with material like this. I <u>doubt</u> that it can be made to come off as a story. By <u>anybody</u>. It would have to be broken up and recast. I don't know how. . . . Basic trouble is structure, depends on our realizing he means what he does to you—and we don't and won't. It's like stories that depend on, posit, Paganini's violin playing, Wilde's wit, Socrates' thinking—and how do you <u>show</u> it to the reader? What I think anyway. I may be wrong, as Fr Urban wd say. My revisions, need I say, are meant well.

Still absorbed in the story, he later sent me another piece of criticism, suggesting how the characters could be made to represent something greater than themselves:

I'd make the girl who says on page 1 "Get off if you're through" the one he later lives with in Spain (make her Spanish, make her Spain, right from the start, in England), so as to keep her in the story, and not just as a good but irrelevant joke, and make the old nursing home Englishwoman England, as I suggested before, but also an early appearance in the story. . . . But what the hell, you can see what I'd do, and chances are, though, you'll appreciate what I'd be after—form, economy.

In the end Jim advised me to do what he'd do—burn it. But eager to see my first story in print, I incorporated all his suggestions, greatly improved it, and published it in *Arizona Quarterly*.

While I tried to look after his secular affairs, Jim interested himself in my spiritual as well as literary welfare. He felt I was on dangerous ground when I moved to Berkeley. He'd once visited San Francisco, but saw only the downtown and was not impressed. He wasn't prepared (he said) for the insubstantiality of the buildings and for "all the houses on top of garages." He made no distinction between San Francisco and Los Angeles, and insisted that California represented "what's wrong with America."

I loved to tease Jim. Visiting a friend who worked in a Catholic rectory and had befriended the parish priest, I found in her house some precious gold-embroidered ecclesiastical robes, made by hand in Belgium, which church "reforms" had eliminated. I couldn't resist dressing up as a bishop and sending Jim the photographs. He responded: "The photo of you in vestments is something else and I only hope if you convert you won't write a book about it; however, I don't think you're ready yet, difficult as it must be for you theologically, being nowhere and/or in California. . . . You're all in my prayers, for what that's worth, damn little in your opinion, I'd guess, but you could be wrong." His work made it clear that he disliked careerist go-getters in the Catholic hierarchy. He made a wry comment on my ambitious attitudes and paid me a backhanded compliment when he remarked that I'd make a good monsignor but would never become a bishop. There was a precedent, I said, in the Jewish-born archbishop of Paris, Cardinal Lustiger.

III

I sent Jim all my books and essays, which often inspired his perceptive, idiosyncratic comments on the authors I wrote about. He himself was a great comic writer, who valued the local and particular as well as the universal. He felt that Nabokov's *Lectures on Literature* had "missed some of the comedy in Joyce. (And probably in Waugh, I'd think, or Beerbohm. . . . Nabokov, as a continental European, had a formal approach to comedy—I think of the M. Hulot movies now. And this isn't done, on the highest level, in the British Isles. Take a book like [the Grossmiths'] DIARY OF A NOBODY—continentals would have killed the material or made it universal and thus lost its special-ness.)"

He liked Joyce's "Counterparts" and "Ivy Day in the Committee Room" far better than the "The Dead," which he felt was flawed by a long prelude before the final revelation. He had, of course, read *A Portrait of the Artist*, "though it wasn't and isn't for me as interesting as DUBLINERS, to say nothing of ULYSSES. I re-read it a year or so ago and found it wanting even more than I'd thought (since I'd read it back in the 30s.) (Last week I saw a marvelous movie of [*Ulysses*], done by Joseph Strick; one of the best movies I've ever seen.)"

Evelyn Waugh, among contemporary writers, was his great hero. Waugh had favorably reviewed Jim's first book, *Prince of Darkness* (1947), in the *Month* and Jim had reviewed *The Loved One* (1948) in *Commonweal*. Waugh—fourteen years older—had influenced Jim, but there was mutual respect on both sides. In 1949, during a lecture tour in America, Waugh had stopped to see him in St. Paul, and Jim's wife, Betty, served crab Newburg. (Waugh invited them to visit him in England "for a limited time," and later Jim and a priest friend went to Piers Court, his home in Gloucestershire.) Waugh inscribed several books and wrote in *Helena* (his most pious and least-read work), "Bet you one dollar you won't finish this." A friend of Jim's, who wrote for a newspaper, asked him to arrange an interview with Waugh. "Do you want me to do this as a favor to you?" Waugh asked Jim plaintively, and was glad to be relieved of this duty. Exhausted by his American journey, Waugh seemed more interested in food and wine than in serious discussion. Having expected a great deal from Waugh, Jim was disappointed by his famed wit and conversation. "I thought you were rough on Waugh," Jim wrote of my review in 1981, defending his mentor. "Accurate, yes, in your statements but wanting in appreciation of Waugh's work and wrong, in my opinion, about his character as a man, despite all the evidence against him." Twelve years later, when I'd come round to his view of Waugh's work, he added, "I'm happy at the higher assessment he seems to be getting from you and others these days."

Though he didn't much like Wyndham Lewis or Hemingway, he had some self-revealing things to say about them: "Lewis may have been the only writer and painter who excelled as both (but was not a *better* writer because he was a painter—my experience with painters as conversationalists and thinkers hasn't been good to date, not that I fancy myself much of either; just know when to shut up)."

His letter on Hemingway, which complemented his blurb for my book, criticized—in cunningly contrived sentences—his lack of a spiritual element: "My feeling is that his built-in shit detector wasn't working too well at times, certainly not toward the end; actually, long before that, maybe even from the start. . . . Still, he was great in his way. My dislike was and is mostly of his philosophy, and that is what makes his end so sad, as it failed him as it naturally would, as it's failed everybody who ever held it."

Jim was extremely helpful when I was writing *Manic Power: Robert Lowell and His Circle* (1987). He was shrewd about Randall Jarrell, sent me copies of his letters from Lowell, and vividly described his friendship with Lowell and Theodore Roethke at Yaddo in 1947—the high point of his literary life. Paraphrasing Revelation 1:8 and T. S. Eliot's *East Coker* ("in my beginning is my end") to describe Jarrell's decline and quoting from my essay on Jarrell's suicide, he observed: "Hard to believe some of the [reviews] could have been done by one so vulnerable, since they are so slashing and funny. . . . His beginning—'collecting money for newspapers and selling Christmas seals'—was his end —'The Certificate of Death . . . lists Jarrell's "Kind of Business or Industry" as "Poetry," ' but he must have thought he could beat the game, the house, though a poet, *as* a poet, without Lowell's name, Frost's face."

Jim was greatly attracted to the big, bearish, larger-than-life Roethke. At Yaddo Ted would knock on Jim's door and shamelessly flatter him by exclaiming he was "the hottest thing in the short story." Then he'd break into a guilty laugh and ask if he could borrow Jim's old car to go into Saratoga Springs for a beer and pastrami sandwich. By day, Ted cheated at croquet by moving his ball. At night he would secretly carry away his liquor bottles and bury them in the lake. Jim loved to recall the competitive and emotionally intense relations of Ted and Cal Lowell (whom Jim never knew in their manic states):

Each did regard the other as a figure of fun, to use your phrase, but not as a "dangerous" one. My feeling is that Ted felt that Cal was too successful with (rather than in) his work—this was 1947, and LORD WEARY'S CASTLE was big. Ted also took the view, and when Cal was present too, that he (Cal) was rather out of it, abstracted, dotty, and liked the line he made up about Cal, frequently quoting it, "Rattleass from Boston, Mass." Ted had spells of disgust (when his face squirmed), but sometimes came up with words that made him feel better, as when after listening for what he considered a long time to [the minor poet] Marguerite Young telling about her inability to get a passport for countries behind the Iron Curtain, he said, "Another mistake of our State Department." Cal enjoyed Ted when he was having one of these spells, as I did—he called me down once, Ted did, "for thinking everything's so funny." In much the same way, Cal was amused by Ted, in and out of his presence, there being no difference as there was, some, where Ted's attitude toward Cal was concerned in and out of his presence—Ted growled and shook his head over Cal's success in the latter case. But Ted was very ambitious, not up to disguising it—like his appetite for food and drink, it just came out. . . . Ted had a rogue quality that he himself seemed to enjoy. The oddest thing, I thought, was that Cal was able to type, and Ted—a good driver of cars—wasn't, so that Cal did a certain amount of that for Ted that summer at Yaddo.

Lowell once ended a heated dispute by asserting the superiority of poets: "We were arguing one night about the respective merits of Faulkner and [Katherine Anne] Porter (I defending her) when Cal, to bring matters to a suitable, acceptable-to-all conclusion, said: 'Well, it's only prose.'"

After visiting Ted in Seattle in 1954, Jim "mostly remembered the steak I was with Ted when he bought, he being a connoisseur of steaks, and being sat down to read his latest work while he hovered about, saying things like 'you fuckin' Catholic, you didn't think I knew stuff like this, did you? Think I'm just a Nature Boy.'"

Jim described Lowell's wife, the novelist Elizabeth Hardwick, as attractive, tough, and ambitious. Jim, close to Senator Eugene McCarthy, also recalled Lowell's friendship with the presidential candidate: "I didn't see much of Lowell and McCarthy when they were close—was invited to join them in Chicago at the convention in '68 but didn't. . . . I think the relationship between them was comradely (what a word, I think, now that I've used it), one of equals who really liked each other for what they were as well as for what they'd done. That, I think, is how it was where I was concerned with each man (and how I think it is with you and me, speaking for myself, anyway)."

We both admired McCarthy. But Jim surprised me by vehemently disagreeing about another Irish-Catholic politician, John Kennedy. Insisting that Kennedy was completely opportunistic and didn't believe in anything, he thought I'd been taken in by his public image. My "greatest fault," according to Jim, was my admiration for Jackie Kennedy. Jim's cynicism, which he was pleased to contrast to my naiveté, extended to the Foreign Service and the much-vaunted presidential "debates." After my daughter had passed the State Department exams and turned down an offer so she could finish law school, Jim remarked, "I think Rachel is wise to stay out of the state department. I always think of them as the faculty, smarter than the administration and the athletic department, but not much." Speaking of the Reagan–Mondale debate in 1984, after which Reagan, in a landslide victory, lost only Minnesota, Jim was less keen on Mondale than I expected. "Isn't anybody here," he wrote irritatedly, "who knows better, going to say so, give some sign, that we're only talking about *shades* of shit?"

IV

Jim's most valuable letters commented, ironically and self-effacingly, on his own work. "You asked," he wrote, "what I thought of [the critic] Martin Green's line on me: as I recall I was coupled with that big O. K. Russian novelist [Mikhail] Sholokhov, I doing for the Church of Rome what he was doing for Moscow, which struck me as, if true, unfair, unless I was to get my dacha in heaven, along with fame."

I taught Jim's stories in my classes on modern literature and appealed to him for insights. When I mentioned that a character in his masterpiece, "Lions, Harts, Leaping Does," had the name of the doubting Apostle Thomas (who was called Didymus, or "twin"), he revealed the background of the story. (John Bale, 1495–1563, converted to Protestantism and became Bishop of Ossory in Ireland. He wrote several literary histories and religious plays, and many bitterly controversial works that attacked the Catholic Church.) Jim wrote:

The name Didymus was chosen for no good reason such as you imagined (reasonably), was the name of an old priest at the highschool I attended. . . . My Didymus does have this doubting quality but only by chance, a lucky break. Othello's "Put out the light" never occurred to me (and doesn't now, as I've forgotten it). The falling snow and canary are as you say and, though you don't say, perhaps too obvious. . . . The opening paragraph, I think, I had simply to suggest that Titus, who'd read it to Didymus was one of the [lame ones] disqualified [for the priesthood], for the irony there might be in that, in view of his superiority, spiritually, to Didymus —this is something where institutions are concerned, and not just the Church, that still fascinates and depresses me, the American presidency being a perennial example [of dud candidates being elected to high office]. . . . Incidentally, the title of "Lions," in case you don't know, which I doubt, comes from St. John of the Cross, "The Spiritual Canticle." Also, incidentally, I ran across Bp Bale in the Newberry Library in Chicago, just by chance—I mention this only to show you that my reading has been random generally and that you would be wrong to think, since I quote Bale, I might be familiar with other writers of the time or, for that matter, with him. The same is true of MORTE D'URBAN, Malory.

When I sent Jim a draft of my essay on "Prince of Darkness" (published in 1986), he made specific corrections as well as general comments about his characters and themes:

Here is where you slip into a gear that isn't quite right, Jeffrey, this talk about spirituality, overdone. It is something that just doesn't often come up, or come to mind, I think, among ordinary priests, oh, maybe at the annual retreat. . . . In short, you are, in a way, like a priest who thinks English professors, off duty, sit around reading the *Oxford Book of English Verse*. . . . I haven't time to re-read the story, or inclination, and don't think it would be a good idea even for the sake of conveying some degree of accuracy I'd want if this were my work, but yours, which it is. I have probably become more tolerant of Fr Burner than I was when I did him. Anyway, it's good and readable, what you've done, and I thank you for doing it.

Jim's carefully wrought inscriptions in my copies of his books threw new light on our friendship as well as on his characters, themes, and textual emendations. In various editions of *Morte D'Urban* he wrote:

—Let Fr Urban be a lesson to you when *you* hit the big time.
—Valerie & Jeffrey Meyers, Honorary Oblates in the Order of St. Clement—Jim Powers (Founder).
—On page 2, line 20, I changed "Fish" to "Jass" in honor of Jelly Roll Morton ("Hello, Central, give me Dr. Jazz")—and unfortunately it shows.

And, after we'd been discussing the Sermon on the Mount:

> —Valerie & Jeffrey Meyers, who have given literary workaholism
> a good name, from one who toiled not and neither did he spin
> if he could help it.

Though Jim was a very private man, he sometimes discussed his private life. He'd been a conscientious objector in World War II and published two early stories about it in the *Catholic Worker*. Later on, he described his time in jail, his grisly work in a hospital, his feelings about the war, his parents' response to his protest, and its influence on him as a writer:

> About my conscientious objection, I was convicted—three years—but was in only 13 months and 23 days, then paroled to a hospital in St. Paul, where I worked as an orderly, which I found tolerable except for the autopsy part, having to beg off that finally, not able to sleep nights thereafter—after an autopsy; I don't know why, only thing like it in my experience to date, not a matter of surgery, blood, etc. Don't attribute it to my feelings about war. Such feelings were long-standing with me, the product of my reading, I having decided long before WWII I wouldn't go that route, which is not to say if, as in Germany, it would have meant beheading, I would've been up to that. I would've gone to c.o. camp if given that choice, which I wasn't. The *Catholic Worker* position was mine, that publication my bible at the time, though I had doubts as to my worthiness. I was more like Auden and Isherwood, I'd say, with lots of misgivings about capitalism and communism, which I continue to have. This whole experience of incarceration confirmed me in this, but I did not suffer greatly, don't think I did, more really from what it meant to my parents, who were not under the ether of my convictions. Mostly it was a waste of time for me, as a writer, though I did get to know people and things I otherwise wouldn't have known.

In the 1980s, describing his daily routine in Minnesota—which was as regular as Immanuel Kant's—he said he got up after nine and remained in his office from eleven to five, six days a week, though he never wrote more than three or four hours a day. On Thursdays he and Betty went shopping in nearby St. Cloud and took care of her aged mother in a nursing home. He had no television and few friends, apart from a sympathetic sculptor, Joe O'Connell, who taught at the nearby women's college, St. Benedict's. Joe created the design for Father Urban's coat-of-arms, which appeared on the title page of Jim's novel.

V

On each of my three later visits to Collegeville I stayed in Jim's house and we talked round the clock. I pieced together the history of his life and heard his views on everything from teaching and writing to money and faith. In August 1984, my wife, eleven-year-old daughter, and I, after spending a year in England, stopped at St. John's on the way back to Colorado.

I was rather shocked, on my first return in daylight, by the primitive conditions in his hair-shirt house, a drab grey stucco dwelling that had originally been built for the workmen who served the monastery. Though Jim and Betty had good food and drink, their deliberately austere life lacked most creature comforts. The bookshelves were rickety, the furniture was shabby (Jim stored his papers in orange crates), there were few rugs and no modern appliances. In the fierce winters the sloping, uninsulated roof and thin walls made it impossible to raise the *inside* temperature above sixty-two degrees, even with the furnace and the fire going full blast. Jim didn't mind the cold, but was sensitive to heat and would never go to a warm place. He fussed with the fans and air conditioner, but (always economical) used them sparingly. A painted wooden sign in the kitchen ambiguously announced, "The pork of today is the bacon of tomorrow." Did it mean the pig was doomed to bacon or destined for a higher end? When I offered to take them out to dinner in St. Cloud, Jim looked quizzical and mordantly asked, "What did I ever do to *you?*"

After an inspection of the church and campus, a tranquil walk around the lake, and a long night's talk, we retired at 2 A.M. Suddenly the silence was shattered. Several pickup trucks loaded with beer kegs and college boys on a weekend reunion had stopped outside the house, and the boys drank and screamed obscenities until 3:30. We conferred on the stairs with an anxious Jim, in his pajamas and clutching a flashlight. He finally called the campus policeman (who did nothing), but refused to complain to the young men, allow me to confront them, or even turn on the houselight to discourage them. Reluctant to provoke them, but embarrassed that his guests and their young daughter had to listen to their filthy language, Jim advised caution. This episode amazed me. By his priestly presence and strong opinions, Jim had impressed me as a forceful personality. But his strength of character co-existed with a physical timidity, a shrinking from direct confrontation that was quite opposite to my own pugnacious temperament.

Jim's father, who was more than a hundred years old, had been a good amateur musician. He'd managed meat-packing plants in dull midwestern cities, like Rockford and Quincy in Illinois, then opened his own grocery store. Unable to buy small quantities at wholesale prices, he'd scoop up specials in supermarkets and sell them for a few cents profit. Inevitably, he went broke. In his teens Jim would go to the South Side of Chicago and come home drunk, but his father never scolded him about this.

He met his wife after her teacher, a nun, asked him if he'd read Betty's unpublished novel. A few days later he proposed to her. They had five children, all born between the late 1940s and late 1950s. I asked him what it was like to have sex without birth control and the responsibility of supporting a family by his writing. He replied, "It was murder." Katherine, who graduated from Boston University and became a library archivist, was married to (and later divorced from) a computer scientist in Cambridge, Massachusetts. The other four children were in Ireland: Mary, a printmaker who lived with the Irish poet Paul Muldoon; James (called "Boz"), married and a painter; Hugh, a photographer who wrote a newspaper column on astronomy; and Jane, who worked in an art gallery. All the children were rather arty; two of them had started and abandoned a doctorate in philosophy; none of them did well financially. Jim helped support his two sons. He had played with his children and read to them, especially from Kenneth Grahame's *The Wind in the Willows*, when they were small. But he didn't have much to do with them once they started school. Betty, the practical one, took care of them and handled the money. He didn't seem particularly close to his children or to his sister in Albuquerque.

Betty—a thin, delicate, capable woman—saved rubber bands, tinfoil, and paper bags. She gardened, baked her own bread, and cooked excellent meals. Proud of her expertise with knives and kitchen utensils, she dismissed the idea of a food processor. She did the laundry practically by hand, managing with an old washer that didn't quite work and rinsing the clothes in the bathtub. She'd never had a job until she began teaching in 1983. Under her own name, Betty Wahl, she'd published a sharp-edged novel—*Rafferty & Co.* (1969)—about their life in Ireland. But Farrar, Straus & Giroux had recently rejected her second work of fiction. She'd just written a third novel, about her childhood and family, which had been with an agent, but inactive, for nearly a year. She lacked the confidence and energy to do anything more about it, and (like Jim) refused my offer to help.

Still weak from recent surgery for cancer of the womb, breasts, and stomach, Betty said stoically, "There's nothing left to cut off." But she was still a pretty woman. She'd managed to keep her hair, despite being "zapped" by chemotherapy, by packing ice around her head. To maintain her precarious health, she had to take many vitamins and hormone supplements, and ate liver to get more iron. Her religion had taught her to accept these agonizing trials, but Jim suffered terribly as he watched her suffer.

They had moved house about thirty times and given away several libraries over the years. Jim liked Ireland best of all and, if he had enough money, would have given up teaching and returned there. But he couldn't get a teaching job in Ireland, and they finally came back to Minnesota, after three long stays outside Dublin, when his sons were ready for college. Betty came from St. Cloud, her mother and brother (a monk) still lived there and, Jim said, "a man always goes to his wife's family."

Hugh had graduated from St. John's, but Boz dropped out. Jim had no attachment to Minnesota, or anywhere else, though he liked its grays and greens. Mocking the fake concept of "neighborliness" in Minnesota, he insisted that the people here were no friendlier than anywhere else. When I remarked, after driving across America, on how different the people and regions seemed to be, Jim said, on the contrary, that they were the same all over.

Jim taught one writing course in the spring term and saw the students individually. He disliked teaching, didn't feel there was much point in it, and said no student of his had ever made it as a writer. He had no academic ambitions and would not accept a better teaching job with a higher salary. But he needed his modest stipend and small house, with heating included. He once accepted an offer to talk for $3,000 and was delighted to cancel the lecture when Betty said they didn't need the money.

He decided to become a writer in high school, partly because he couldn't get a decent job. He didn't have the money for college and didn't think it was worth studying at night to get a degree. He used his first two initials in imitation of T. S. Eliot, whom he greatly admired. With "Lions, Harts, Leaping Does" he'd had the almost sexual thrill of writing fast and "seeing the end of the tunnel." He thought writers drank heavily to achieve a high that released their creative powers rather than to compensate for loneliness, frustration, and failure. His early exhilaration had been replaced by an acute self-consciousness, and writing had now become for him an arduous, torturous task. He lacked self-confidence and was constantly dissatisfied with his own work. He'd recently showed Betty a story and thought the work had failed when she asked, "Does he get the money at the end?" That would have happened after the story ended and was not the point he was trying to make.

He felt quite bitter about Doubleday, which "nearly killed" *Morte D'Urban* after it won the National Book Award in 1963. His agent got him out of his next-book contract with them, and Jim hoped he'd do better with Robert Gottlieb at Knopf. He'd worked for twenty years on his current novel, which was due eight years ago. Every year he wrote a penitential letter and apologized to his editor for the delay.

In 1970, for a book of stories and a novel, he'd received an advance of $30,000, which he thought was quite good. He had a $500 annual retainer from the *New Yorker* and was paid fifty cents a word, or about $3,000 each, for two stories they published in January 1978 and March 1979. But the *New Yorker* had also rejected two other stories—and he felt they were right to do so. In 1948 he'd been successfully recommended for a Guggenheim by Katherine Anne Porter, and didn't feel he had the right to apply for other grants. He was later awarded $25,000 by the Ingram-Merrill Foundation, and would have welcomed a MacArthur fellowship.

Jim lived at St. John's from opportunity, familiarity, and habit, and didn't need daily contact with priests to portray them. He knew the material and could write it anywhere. In contrast to the subject of psychoanalysis, which everyone thought they knew about, it was easy to publish fiction about priests. He'd never wanted to be a priest himself, disliked the responsibilities involved, and couldn't bear talking to old ladies after Mass. Half-ironically, half-literally he exclaimed, "Marxism is the work of the Devil." He thought that priests should hide their doubts about faith, and that in the foreseeable future there could never be married priests in the Catholic Church. That was *the* crucial issue, *the* sacrifice.

When Valerie told him about her fatuous job interview, recorded on tape, at a Jesuit high school in Denver, Jim sympathized and regretfully remarked, "The Church wants to be like everyone else now." He went to Mass with Betty every day, but sat alone with her in the upper balcony. He loathed the recent changes in the ritual—like singing rousing hymns and embracing or shaking hands with your neighbor. These futile attempts to make the service more attractive merely debased and vulgarized the Church. When I said that I envied his faith, he replied that he might actually be as sceptical as I was. He had made the same wager as Pascal. He wanted to believe and hoped that faith would carry him through doubt.

VI

Our second visit to Collegeville took place after Betty's death, in October 1990, on the way to the Harbourfront writers' conference in Toronto. Jim invited Joe O'Connell and his colleague Charles Thornberry, and fussed about while Valerie prepared the dinner. He was working on two books, a memoir and an academic novel, but didn't seem to be making much progress on either of them. He was also anxious about what to do with his battered old possessions—he couldn't sell the furniture and didn't want to throw it away—when he had to move out of the college-owned house after retirement.

By the summer of 1987 Jim had finally completed *Wheat That Springeth Green*, sent it to Knopf (Gottlieb had by then left to edit the *New Yorker*) and hadn't heard from them for a long time. I was then writing a life of Lawrence for Knopf, and urged him to call them collect and find out what was happening. "Oh," he said, scandalized, "I couldn't do that." As with the rowdy students, he refused to assert himself and defend his interests. So I called his new editor, told her he was one of the best writers in America, and urged her to push the book through the press.

"My having finished the novel at long, long last has been pretty well savaged by this great silence," Jim wrote, "and, of course, by Betty's trouble, which has been going on, more or less constantly, since May (this her third stay in hospital since then)." The first printing of *Wheat* was only 8,500 and sold out before the publication date. There were two more printings of 8,500 each, with a month in between when the book was unavailable, and the lost sales had hurt and angered him.

I felt he had also been badly treated by St. John's. It paid him a low salary, gave him a wretched house, and didn't recognize his stature in the literary world. When forced to accept an honorary degree, he expressed a rare complaint: "Typical, my role here, in this matter, of my life, as I usually see it, trial by crap. What I get for not being like you and Hemingway"—though he certainly didn't *want* to be like either of us. I urged St. John's to sponsor a conference to commemorate his seventieth birthday, but nothing came of it. He was grateful for my encouragement and efforts on his behalf, but always tried to stop them. When I phoned him on his seventy-fifth birthday and asked what celebrations were taking place, he paused for a moment and then said, ". . . your call."

When I suggested that an interview in the *Paris Review* "Writers at Work" series would enhance his reputation, he replied that I could stay with him whenever I liked but, "here my Norman cunning comes out—no interviews. I'm sick of quacking for publication and, with no new book to justify it, will not perform." When *Wheat* was shortlisted for the National Book Award, he gave only one reading, at the University Club in St. Paul. He wanted to be a widely read author whose books would make readers burst out laughing. But, he wrote, "I no longer (if I ever did, in my heart) believe there is any hope for me as a popular author, even a literary one, and so it's not as you think, indifference to my career, but simply recognizing reality for what it must be for me." When I quoted Mencken on the fate, despite their universal themes, of regional writers—"I don't care how well [Cather] writes. I don't give a damn what happens in Nebraska"—Jim smiled knowingly.

Betty had been seriously ill since 1973. After a ghastly struggle with cancer, she died in 1988, and her loss had left a great wound in Jim's heart. He'd gone to Mass every day and "prayed like mad for her." I didn't ask, though I wanted to, why his prayers went unanswered and why a good woman had to suffer so terribly. He did write, however, "I often think of Sylvia Plath's [childhood remark after her father's death] 'I'll never speak to God again,' since reading it in your Lowell book." Betty asked that "St. James Infirmary" be played at her funeral, not only because he loved jazz, but also because James had turned her bedroom into an infirmary and had cared for her with sweet devotion. We visited her grave, which still didn't have a headstone. Joe O'Connell, absorbed in his massive sculpture—"the size of Mount Rushmore"—for a Catholic church in Las Vegas, hadn't gotten around to it.

Referring to St. John's sister college, Jim said that Betty "had bought the St. Benedict's line" on having a large family and then felt she'd been trapped by it. Though he seemed to have been a devoted husband, he was remorseful about the way he'd treated her. He felt guilty about ignoring Betty—his "Indian shadow"—when they were at Yaddo, and about spending all his time with his literary cronies, Roethke and Lowell. Betty didn't fit in there, and he'd not been too concerned about her happiness. He agonized about not having paid enough attention to her wishes and needs, and felt he'd been too critical and selfish. He had no one to talk to now about the events of the day or much weightier matters. He grieved for many years, and had already bought his grave plot next to hers. "With Betty gone," he observed, "a lot of my questions go unanswered, unasked rather, for they're mostly unanswerable." Though lonely and not at all pleased with his reclusive life, he felt a second marriage would place him in an absurd position. One colleague, separated from her husband, asked if she could rent a room in his house: an impossible idea. A Hispanic woman in New Jersey had written him a fan letter, and he met her when he went to New York to receive a $1,500 literary prize.

Betty's death was followed by a series of Job-like ordeals that made Jim withdraw from his friends into negation, depression, and creative sterility. In my copy of *Wheat* he poignantly wrote, "I've been silent, forgive me." A poor hand at household repairs, in 1991 he fell and hurt his back while trying to install an air conditioner. The intense pain when he sat prevented him from working. But he refused to see doctors, whom he profoundly mistrusted. The following year, never before seriously ill but now aged seventy-five, Jim began to have prostate and kidney problems. Friends told him he'd lost a lot of weight, looked terrible, and needed medical help. But he waited till he urinated blood and then couldn't urinate at all before driving himself to the emergency room in the middle of the night. "Poisons had backed up" into his kidneys and permanently damaged his vital organs, and he now looked old and weak. His voice had become faint, he found it rather difficult to speak, and he compared himself to a ventriloquist's dummy. He couldn't work while a "patient," and was continually distracted by visits to the dreaded doctors, who devised horrific treatments and put in a catheter. He hadn't even asked if he had cancer (he didn't) until he'd been in hospital for several days. "Don't mess with your kidneys," he warned me, and admitted he'd been "stupid about medical matters."

But the cup had not yet passed. In 1991 Betty's mother, aged ninety-one, was expected to die at any moment. Sean O'Faolain, his last close friend in Ireland, had passed away that year. Katherine, in Cambridge, had recovered from breast cancer, but her sister Mary had developed the same disease. She'd called it asthma, told no one and—because of what happened to Betty—chose to die rather than endure a long, painful, and perhaps futile series of treatments. Still recovering from kidney disease, Jim went over to Ireland to say farewell to Mary just before the end. But, heavily sedated with morphine, she could not discuss her illness and impending death. Now that Jim had retired from teaching, there was no longer any reason to remain in Collegeville, but he would not move to be near his children in Massachusetts or Ireland. He feared he owed long-standing taxes to the Irish government and couldn't go to Ireland—or anywhere else.

VII

Our third and final visit, again en route to Harbourfront, took place four years later, in October 1994. Rousing himself for the occasion, Jim seemed glad to see us. Witty and hospitable, though now more subdued, he praised my work and my second lecture at St. John's.

His old dwelling had been torn down by the university while he was in hospital, and he had moved into an even smaller and uglier, more primitive and uncomfortable house, just up the road. Built in the 1940s, when he first began to write, it had never been remodeled and looked like an old rooming house in a grade-B film. He found the move and readjustment very difficult, the rent too high, the plumbing antique. After the toilet was flushed, it took about ten minutes to fill up. The slightest movement could be heard throughout the house. But Jim, as usual, preferred to suffer rather than discuss the problems with his farmer-handyman landlord. He insisted we take his bed and slept on a cot in the damp basement.

Jim had about twenty-five bottles of liquor, many of them very old and with only a few dregs left in them, lined up on a precarious shelf in the archaic kitchen. Below the shelf, in an open coat rack, he hung up the shirts he had ironed himself. He still had many bottled preserves Betty had made, and was careful to give Valerie good food to cook. But we recoiled at some revolting smelly cheese that he insisted, in his thrifty way, was still edible. At dinner he drank a beer and a third of a bottle of wine. He disliked household chores but, with monklike penitence, did his laundry in the rusty bathtub, on his knees. He typed his work on a low table in the smallest room of the house (the only warmish place in winter), near a row of books signed by Waugh and Lowell, Flannery O'Connor and Peter Taylor.

His literary papers, once organized by his daughter Katherine, had lapsed into a chaotic state. He'd had offers to buy them, but didn't want to part with them during his lifetime. He considered them his main legacy to his children and resisted the idea of a valuation by a librarian at the University of Minnesota.

He didn't have an agent or contract for his next book and didn't want to increase the pressure on himself by getting them. He wouldn't take an advance—he'd only have to pay more taxes. Though he had an accountant, he was afraid of the IRS and wouldn't take a (perfectly valid) deduction for the office in his house. He received only about $60 a month from his college pension, but wasn't interested in buying anything and had enough money for his all-too-modest needs. He really hated and feared materialism and "couldn't live in a house where the bathroom worked."

His twenty-two-year-old Chrysler, a perfect complement to the house, seemed to have more rust on it than metal. He could have used a new four-wheel-drive for the deep snows and harsh winters, but refused to buy one. He had to repair the old car for a rare ninety-minute journey to St. Paul, at the invitation of Eugene McCarthy and Garrison Keillor, to rename a theater after a local hero, Scott Fitzgerald.

It was hard to pin Jim down on his daily routine. He tried to begin writing by late morning, worked as long as he could, and often did no work at all. Blocked but not, he claimed, depressed (at least while we were there), he lacked the impulse to finish the work—the "orgasmic feeling" of knowing what he wanted to write and how to perfect it. He wouldn't publish his fiction merely because he was able to do so. He had written 20,000 words of a new novel but hadn't shown it to anyone—wouldn't even show it to a writer, like Saul Bellow, whom he respected. He'd known Bellow at the University of Minnesota and found him a stimulating and sympathetic companion. It was amazing that a writer as good as Bellow ever managed to win the Nobel Prize.

Jim disliked walking and drove quite short distances on campus. When we protested that he needed exercise to stay healthy, he insisted that he had a method of his own: pulling on ropes while lying in bed. He now watched golf and baseball on television, and the news every night while he ate dinner. He believed racial conflict was one of the main reasons why life in America would soon become intolerable. He kept up with current magazines—*TLS, American Scholar, New Yorker*— but found books a distraction and rarely read them. He praised Martin Amis's *London Fields* and Mary Gordon's *Final Payments,* and said that Gordon's Jewish father had publicly proselytized after his conversion to Catholicism. He'd sent his son Hugh, a serious student of philosophy, an article by Roger Scruton in the *New Criterion,* but had offended Hugh by thinking he'd be interested in such a trivial piece. He compared himself and Hugh to Robert Frost and his son Carol. Both fathers were well intentioned, but did the wrong thing.

Jim visited the sick and, no longer praying for Betty's recovery, attended Mass only on Sunday. He'd heard from a priest who'd seen the Pope in Ireland that His Holiness, speaking English with the same accent Joseph Conrad must have had, talked too much and far too long. Jim thought someone—perhaps a cardinal—should have told him to shut up.

In everyday speech Jim used old-fashioned expressions like "in spades" and "he was murder." Despite his acute intelligence, he was still unworldly and a bit naive. When I mentioned Frost's sly remark— "to a husband the stork was worse than the cuckoo"—he missed the point. This simplicity made him teasable. In Collegeville, which had no shops, I discovered just before my lecture that the sole of my shoe was detached from the upper and flapping about. When I asked Jim how I could repair it, he eagerly fetched his own glue, hammer, and nails. With furrowed brow and great concentration, he smoothed on layers of adhesive and pounded in a small mountain of metal. Proud of his handiwork, he said "that ought to do it" and we resumed our conversation. After a time, as we sat talking, I glanced down at the shoe and casually remarked, "I'm afraid the sole's come loose again." Jumping up from his chair, he knelt down, examined my footgear—and realized he'd been bit!

Though Jim didn't like living alone, he also disliked most social life. He didn't attend cultural events on campus and preferred to be on his own. When I warned him that he was becoming a hermit, he said there was no one to talk to but Joe O'Connell—and was devastated when Joe died in 1995. Since everything had already been said, Jim had no choice but to remain silent. "I don't know about being here [in Minnesota], or anywhere else, as making much difference," he wrote in his last letter to me. "I live here, as I did in Ireland, though in more ignorance here of the outside world, newspapers being what they are here and broadcasting, the guiding principle being not to make morons and illiterates feel left out. . . . Which takes me back to the problem of me as hermit. The truth is I love a big time and have become a hermit by default." Thinking, perhaps, of *King Lear*'s "As flies to wanton boys, are we to the gods; / They kill us for their sport," he was troubled by having to kill flies in his office. Too stupid to escape through the hole in his screen, they came to represent for him the human condition.

Index

Index